has achieved this aim or not must be left to others to judge.

All available books have been freely used, some of which have proved very serviceable. Grateful acknowledgment is here made of the clear suggestions and wise criticisms of a personal friend, Dr. W. J. Erdman.

WILLIAM G. MOOREHEAD.

PREFACE

This little book is not a commentary on the Revelation; it does not aspire to such a dignity. It is designed to be just what its title announces— studies in the Revelation. For years the writer has deeply felt the lack of a satisfactory analysis of this book and a reasonable and helpful solution of its mysterious and marvellous structure. Reading it, as he has done, through a rather long life, he confesses he saw little or no connection between the various parts, he understood nothing scarcely of the articulation of its Visions, nor saw any definite, far-reaching plan running through it and binding its strange members into a harmonious and majestic unity. The studies of some months past, rather years, have served to open much of what for long was almost sealed and to pour light into many a dark place. The chief aim of this Study is to help the reader and student of the Apocalypse into an apprehension of the plan and the design of this great Scripture. Whether the writer

COPYRIGHTED, 1908

BY

THE UNITED PRESBYTERIAN BOARD OF
PUBLICATION

PITTSBURGH, PA.

STUDIES

IN THE

Book of Revelation

" Other men laboured, and ye are entered into
their labours "

BY

WILLIAM G. MOOREHEAD, D.D., LL.D.

Professor in Xenia Theological Seminary

PITTSBURGH, PA.

UNITED PRESBYTERIAN BOARD
OF PUBLICATION

English
Français
Deutsche
Italiano
Español
Português

www.forgottenbooks.com

Mythology Photography **Fiction**
Fishing Christianity **Art** Cooking
Essays Buddhism Freemasonry
Medicine **Biology** Music **Ancient
Egypt** Evolution Carpentry Physics
Dance Geology **Mathematics** Fitness
Shakespeare **Folklore** Yoga Marketing
Confidence Immortality Biographies
Poetry **Psychology** Witchcraft
Electronics Chemistry History **Law**
Accounting **Philosophy** Anthropology
Alchemy Drama Quantum Mechanics
Atheism Sexual Health **Ancient History**
Entrepreneurship Languages Sport
Paleontology Needlework Islam
Metaphysics Investment Archaeology
Parenting Statistics Criminology
Motivational

1 MONTH OF FREE READING

at

www.ForgottenBooks.com

By purchasing this book you are eligible for one month membership to ForgottenBooks.com, giving you unlimited access to our entire collection of over 1,000,000 titles via our web site and mobile apps.

To claim your free month visit:

www.forgottenbooks.com/free442265

ISBN 978-1-332-77634-4
PIBN 10442265

CONTENTS.

THE REVELATION

CHAPTER I

AUTHORSHIP AND DATE.

The study of this great prophecy is entered upon with much diffidence; almost with hesitation. Many regard it as so abstruse and obscure that any satisfactory interpretation of it is extremely difficult, if not hopeless. Only great scholars and lifelong students of the Bible are competent, it is thought, to deal with its profound mysteries, and even these are often baffled by its symbolism, and defeated by its depths. Others should not attempt its elucidation. Such is the feeling of many.

Notwithstanding the difficulties, its study is imposed on all Christians. It is a part of the word of God. It bears the name and authority of the Lord Jesus Christ. Its august title is, " The Revelation of Jesus Christ which God gave to him to show unto his servants." It is an Apocalypse, an unveiling of what could not be otherwise known. It is for the instruction, guidance, and comfort of God's people.

The prophet Daniel was bidden to " shut up the vision," to " shut up the words, and seal the book, even to the time of the end " (Dan. viii: 26; xii: 4, 9). But our Lord's command to John is: "What thou seest, write in a book, and send it to the seven churches," i: 11. The instruction of the revealing angel to the Seer when he is bringing the mighty visions of the prophecy to an end is, " Seal not up the words of the prophecy of this book; for the time is at hand," xxii: 10. Explicitly the Saviour declares, " I Jesus have sent mine angel to testify unto you these things for the churches," xxii: 16. The Revelation, therefore, is for the whole people of God; to them it is an unsealed book, and it is intended to be their teacher and their guide in things that very vitally concern them.

Furthermore, a special blessing is promised to him who reads and to them who " hear the words of the prophecy, and keep the things that are written there-in," i: 3. The public reading of the book in the assemblies of Christians is here recognized, which places it on the same plane with the other books of Scripture. Its Divine Author is thus at pains to exalt its importance, to commend its teachings, and to promise a rich reward for its study. Among the last words in the Bible is this gracious encourage-ment to the diligent student of the Apocalypse: " Be-hold, I come quickly; blessed is he that keepeth the words of the prophecy of this book," xxii: 7. To keep these words one must know them; to know them one must ponder them, and fill his mind with their deep teachings. They make a grievous mistake who look on the book as enigmatical, incomprehensible; or who, if granting it may be in measure understood, stigmatize it as impractical and profitless; as having little, if any, bearing on the believer's life. Let us turn to the book.

I. Who was its penman? Four times he called himself John, i: 1, 4, 9; xxii: 8. There is no description of him beyond his name, no word is there to indicate what John it was to whom the writing of the Apocalypse was committed. But it is not difficult to identify him. There is but one John to whom we would naturally suppose the Lord would entrust such a work, the John so intimately associated with Him during His earthly ministry, the " Beloved Disciple," the near friend of Jesus; John the apostle. There is scarcely any doubt but that the writer was this John, or one who sought to pass for him. We may at once put aside the notion of fraud or imposture. The spirit of holiness and truth which pervades every page of the book is incompatable with the spirit of falsehood. The internal evidence overwhelmingly supports this view. That a forger should write such a book as this is simply incredible.

Moreover, the unanimous testimony of the Christian Church of the second century by its chief teachers strengthens this conclusion. But few witnesses need here be introduced. Justin Martyr (c. A. D. 150) expressly affirms that John, " one of the apostles of Christ," was the writer of the Revelation. Justin was probably born within a few years of John's death, or even while John was living, and he bore this witness within fifty years of John's demise. It is not likely Justin could be mistaken touching so vital a matter, nor that the source of his information was not thoroughly trustworthy. Irenaeus (c. 180) apparently never heard of any other than John the apostle as the writer. Irenaeus' testimony is of the utmost value, for he was " the grand-pupil of John," as Dr. Whedon describes him; he was the disciple of Polycarp, and Polycarp was the disciple of John, so that between John and Irenaeus there stands but one, the sainted Polycarp, Bishop of Smyrna and martyr of Christ, and intimate companion of John himself. The Muratori Canon (c. A. D. 170), Melito of Sardis (c. A. D. 180), Tertullian the great Latin Father, and many others bear the like witness to the genuineness of the Apocalypse. If credence is to be put in the unanimous testimony of antiquity, if historical evidence is worth anything in deciding a historical date and the authorship of a book, it seems to be decided by unimpeachable witnesses that the apostle John was the writer of this book.

But why does John suppress his name in the Gospel and in the epistles and record it here? Because the Revelation is pre-eminently prophecy, and every prophetic writing is authenticated by the name of the prophet. The prophets of the Old Testament invariably attach their names to their books, because their names are a guarantee of their predictions. John opens the Apocalypse with the announcement of his own name, and of the source and aim of his prophecies, precisely as do the Old Testament prophets.

II. The date of the book is a matter of almost bitter controversy. Two widely differing dates compete for the mastery. Each characterizes a school of interpreters, and each is advocated and defended with great zeal, and in some instances with violence. These dates are, respectively, A. D. 68, and A. D. 95-6. The first affirms that the book was written when Galba was Emperor of Rome, the other when Domitian was reigning. The adoption of either of these dates determines almost exclusively one's interpretation of the book. If the earlier is accepted as true, then one of necessity must accept what is commonly known as the preterist interpretation, namely, that the predictions contained herein had, and were expected to have their fulfilment in John's own time, that chaps i-xix, particularly, relate to the persecutions of Nero, the fall of Jerusalem, the dismemberment of the Jewish nation and the dispersion of Israel among the nations of the world. If the second date is assumed to be the correct one, then the Revelation has little or nothing to do with the events referred to, for it lies this side of them by a quarter of a century.

A. D. 68 is advocated by many writers of great learning and keen, critical acumen. Historical evidence for it there is none till centuries after the book was written. The first writer to mention an early date is Epiphanius, about A. D. 365, but his statement is of no value, for he says that John wrote the Apocalypse in the reign of the emperor Claudius, *i. e.*, about A. D. 50-54, and he makes the incredible assertion that at the time John was ninety years old, whereas, in point of fact he could hardly have been above fifty. If Epiphanius had named Domitian as

the emperor, he would have been in exact accord with
Irenaeus, who affirms that it was written near the close
of Domitian's reign, *i. e.,* A. D. 90-96, at which time
the apostle would be about ninety. Some even suppose
that Domitian and not Claudius is meant, but the
blunderer, as Epiphanius is known to be, twice wrote
the wrong name. He is the only witness for an early
date among the primitive writers, and his testimony is
a huge mistake.

A. D. 68 rests almost exclusively on internal evidence. Language and style are pressed into its support. Dionysius of Alexandria (3d cent.), argued
from these, that he who wrote the Fourth Gospel and
1 John did not write the Revelation, for the language
and style employed in the latter forbid the belief that
its author also wrote the other books ascribed to
John. Dionysius has been followed by multitudes
since, whose main argument is, John may have written
Revelation, but if he did it was early in his life, when
he did not know Greek as he came to know it when an
older man; and so he may have written this book at 68
A. D., and the Gospel about A. D. 80-90. We may
dismiss the point without further remark.

Chap. xi: 1, 2, 8, seems to affirm that Jerusalem
was standing and the Temple was still existing when
the book was written. But it may as conclusively
be affirmed that it is Jerusalem rebuilt and reinhabited
by Hebrews, as that the Beast and the two witnesses
of the same chapter have never yet appeared in history. Whedon well says, " The use of Jerusalem and
temple and tribes as apocalyptic symbols no more

proves the literal existence of the city than the description of Babylon proves that that great capital then existed in all its power and glory." The advocacy of this early date mainly arises out of the interpretation of the book. All who hold it teach that these prophecies relate to events near John's own time, that they sprang from the conditions then existing, and are addressed to his contemporaries. Accordingly, the interpretation governs the date, and then the date is made to rule the interpretation, a vicious method which has no real worth. It is believed that Nero was " The Beast," that he did not die by his own hand, but that he was almost fatally wounded, but was hidden by friends, that he concealed himself in Parthia, his "deadly wound " being healed, and that in due time he would reappear at the head of a great army, destroy Rome, annihilate Christianity, deliver Israel from all foes, glorify Jerusalem, and become the Antichrist, the mock Messiah. Such was the vague rumor floating about over the empire about A. D. 68, and John accepted it, and wrote the Apocalypse with this hypothesis dominating him. The seven heads on the Beast are explained to signify Roman Emperors, viz.: Augustus, Tiberius, Caligula, Claudius, Nero, the " five fallen" (xvii: 10) ; the sixth is Galba (" the one is "), and the seventh, Galba's successor, was to be Nero restored, the Man of Sin, the Antichrist. Such is the rationalistic view of Revelation, and it is supported by its advocates by vast research and acute reasoning.

Now, if the Apocalypse was actually based on the

foundation just described, then, in less than ten years historical events and facts proved the book to be totally mistaken, false, and untrustworthy.   For Nero did not reappear, the seventh head of the Beast did not become Antichrist, Rome did not fall; instead, Jerusalem did, and Israel, instead of being delivered and exalted, went into an exile that still endures.   Could any book, specially one claiming to be a revelation from God, survive such an overwhelming defeat— such utter bankruptcy of its essential contents? Yet the book lived, and has continued to live to this day. We may dismiss both the hypothesis and the date from further consideration.   Unhesitatingly we accept Irenaeus' date, viz.: near the close of Domitian's reign, A. D. 90-96.   Many whose judgment on this point is of the highest worth accept, in part, or wholly, this date, *e. g.*, Ramsay, Orr, Harnack, Swete. " Critical opinion appears to be steadily returning to the traditional date," *i. e.*, 90-96 (Purves).

CHAPTER II.

SYMBOLISM.

III. Symbolism. Every reader is impressed with the extraordinary imagery of the book. Other prophetic Scripture exhibits the same peculiarity, as Isaiah, Ezekiel, Daniel, Zechariah, even the Pentateuch has it in some degree. But this is a book of symbols; a series of gorgeous pictures which begin with the opening chapter and continue to the end. A marvellous profusion of this pictorial representation characterizes it. Some of the symbols are easily understood, for their meaning shines through the drapery that covers the great thought, but others are so complex, so unearthly, and portentous in their vastness and mysteriousness as to daze, overwhelm us. But let us be persuaded of this, that whether we can read the enigma, the deep idea hidden in the symbol or not, the idea is there all the same, and it is the supreme duty of the expositor to toil on at it till he uncover its meaning, at least partially. Let some features of the symbolism be noted:

(a) The imagery is taken from the Old Testament. In chap. i, the dress and posture of the glorified Son of Man, the candlesticks amid which He walks, are from the Temple, from Israel's high priest, and from the candlestick of the sanctuary. The four living creatures of chap. iv are taken from the Pentateuch and Ezekiel. The Beast of chap. xiii is already in Daniel vii. The harvest of xiv: 14-16, and the vintage of xiv: 17-20 are in Joel iii, and in Zech. xiv, while the last worldwide conflict, xix, is described in Dan. vii, xi, xii; in Zeph., in Joel, Zech. and Matt. xxiv. We might go on to see that the Revelation, as a whole, is bound up with the earlier prophetic Scriptures by the closest and most intimate ties. Indeed, as one studies this relation of the two Testaments to each other in type, symbol, language, thoughts and expressions, he is profoundly struck with the unity of the Bible, and particularly with the oneness of the great prophetic themes of the holy word.

John lays all Scripture under tribute, and draws from it much, if not all his material. Numbers furnished by another may serve to make this plain. Revelation consists of 404 verses, of which 265 verses contain O. T. language, while there are 550 references to it (Prof. Swete gives 278 verses). The Greek texts of Wescott and Hort, and of Nestle, exhibit its use of the O. T. by printing the borrowed words and phrases in a different type. On a single page of Nestle's small volume no less than twenty such words and phrases have been counted. The Revelation gathers into itself the imagery, language, and objects of the older prophecies, and to know the full mind of the Spirit the student must go back to the source for light and guidance.

All this shows how intimately the prophetic parts of the Bible are united, and how one must take his principles of interpretation from the whole word of

God. To attempt to interpret the book by heathen customs and Gentile habits and history is fatal to the right understanding of it. It is strictly Biblical; it moves within the circle of the prophets of God; it is saturated with Hebrew modes of thought, and is filled and thrilled with Hebrew hopes and assurances. John thinks in Hebrew, writes in the style of a Hebrew prophet, and speaks with the authority of a Hebrew Seer.

(b) Progress marks Biblical prophecy. Daniel's predictions advance beyond those of Isaiah, of Joel, and even of Ezekiel. Zechariah adds features to the growing picture of the End-time, and of the mighty struggle between the Kingdom of God and the kingdom of Satan, which none of the prophets who preceded him have foretold. Jesus in the Olivet prophecy, Matt. xxiv, xxv, Luke xxi, fills into it details, and features, and lines, which make it far more specific, clear, intelligible, and graphic; while Paul, in 2 Thess., with a few strokes of the prophetic pencil, paints the Man of Sin so vividly and so frightfully, as that the monster when he comes will be recognized instantly by the people of God. But the Apocalypse crowns the whole prophetic word with its symbols and pictures, its explanations and its solemn testimonies, its four great series of sevens, all leading to the consummation, to the Advent and the Victory, so that the man of God is furnished an infallible guide for the perilous times that are fast approaching

While the Apocalypse is the final and by far the fullest revelation of the " Things to come," it is not

2

an independent prophecy, nor is it disconnected with the earlier disclosures of the future which God has been pleased to give us. On the contrary, the book gathers into itself all that precedes it in the same great field, but adds thereto, and unfolds, and reveals more and more, till the colossal portrait, in all its awful features, stands complete.

With two great prophecies the Revelation is most closely and indissolubly bound up, namely, Daniel's and the Lord's Olivet Discourse. How intimately the book of Daniel and the book of Revelation are connected every careful reader of the Bible well knows. The supreme subjects, the times, the opposing forces, and the issue of the mighty conflict are in both identical. In both the same theme is prominent, viz.: the Kingdom of God in its deadly struggle with the hostile world-power and its victory over it. Daniel and John are companion books, at once complemental and supplemental of each other. The Lord's Olivet Discourse, as recorded in Matt. xxiv, and Luke xxi, furnishes a sort of frame for much of the Apocalypse. It is beyond dispute that Christ deals with two supreme events, viz.: the Fall of Jerusalem and His Second Advent. It is with the latter event He mainly is concerned. He speaks with much fulness on the closing scenes of the age, of the Tribulation, the signs that announce the nearness of the Advent, and of the Advent itself. It is with the same great crisis of the world that our book deals. In Daniel it is the Gentile World-power, become apostate and hostile to God and His cause and people, that is crushed by the overwhelming judgment of the Lord. The same monstrous Power, beastly and savage, reappears in the Revelation, and meets there the same tremendous doom. In the Olivet Prophecy of Christ the people of Israel hold a pre-eminent place; and in the Revelation the same chosen people are alike conspicuous. It is not too much to say that the Apocalypse is the expansion, with marvellous additions, of the Olivet Prophecy and the book of Daniel. He who studies both these until he comes to understand them will find the study of our book greatly facilitated.

CHAPTER III.

SYSTEMS OF INTERPRETATION.

IV. Systems of Interpretation. Four methods of interpreting the book are advocated, which we describe as briefly as possible.

The first is that commonly called *Preterism,* to which reference has already been made. Its fundamental principle is this: the Revelation is a dramatic representation of conditions and events existent in John's own day, that its visions must be limited to his horizon, that it has to do with the Roman State, with Israel, Jerusalem, and the Christian Church of the first century, the apostolic age, and with the conflicts then raging. It holds that Nero was the Beast, that the letters of his name written in Hebrew (Nero Cæsar) give the mystic number 666; that John adopted the absurd fiction, that Nero did not die by his own hand, that he was somewhere concealed till the hour should arrive for his reappearance, when most extraordinary things would take place. This, in short, is the rationalistic interpretation which obviously destroys the credibility of the book and reduces it to the level of the wildest fable.

There are those, however, who are evangelical in their belief, who accept the book as an authoritative revelation, but who adopt the preterist explanation. Among these may be mentioned the most recent writers; as, *e. g.,* Prof. Ramsay (Letters to the Seven Churches, 1905), Dr. Swete (Apocalypse of St. John, 1907, 2d ed.), and Simcox (Cambridge Series of Comm.). They hold that John did actually accept the fiction about Nero, and that he used it to make his teaching effective and illustrative. Both Ramsay and Swete date the book in the reign of Domitian, A. D. 95-6, and they think that Nero's " deadly wound was healed" when the fierce persecutor of the Christians, Domitian, became Emperor. They hold that Domitian, A. D. 81-96, was the Beast of xiii, and Babylon the Harlot City of Rome, xvii. These writers have poured a flood of light on the times and the conditions of the apostolic age; in this respect, as in others also, their books are genuinely helpful. But we believe their exposition of the Revelation utterly breaks down when confronted with the facts in the case. John distinctly tells us that five of the heads of the Beast had fallen (of course when he wrote), that one, the sixth, was existing at the time, and that there was to come the seventh head of the monster, when the mighty events which he was foretelling would be accomplished (xvii: 10). But Domitian was not the seventh head of the Beast, nor the eighth, as this view necessitates he should be. No less than five Emperors ruled between Nero and Domitian, viz.: Galba, Otho, Vitellius, Vespasian, and Titus. Even if the first three of these be thrown out because of their short reigns, still two others remain, one of whom was Emperor for ten years and the other for two. Besides, none of the stupendous events predicted in the book, as occurring when the Beast is here, took place under any of these Emperors, nor have they to this day, in the judgment of many scholars. The defect of these preterist views is mainly this: a totally inadequate recognition of the inspiration of the book. One who really believes that Jesus Christ gave this revelation to John in Patmos, as John solemnly affirms He did (i: 1-11), cannot for a moment accept the notion that John adopted the fiction about Nero, or that he fancied the visions shown him were being fulfilled in the conditions which surrounded him. Christ's glorious Advent is the center and sum of this book, not John's own times, and not till He comes will its supreme predictions be realized.

The second system of interpretation is the *Spiritual.* By this is meant that the book treats of the conflict between good and evil, between Christ and Satan, the conflict that began with man's sin and fall, that runs through all history, and that will end only with the end of time. The Revelation is a poetic and prophetic picture of the struggle between righteousness and sin, and that accordingly we are not to look for special fulfilments of its predictions; it deals with great principles, with their action, and with their defeats and victories. So the Seals are intended to show one phase of the conflict, the Trumpets another, and the Vials a third—all these are but vivid photographs of the war between good and evil, not specific transactions.

The objections to this interpretation are conclusive, we think. (1.) There is its novelty, to begin with.

The ancient Church did not so regard the book; nor did the Church of the Middle Ages; nor did that of the Reformation; nor has it in later times. Few, indeed, even in our own day accept it. It is advocated, however, by some very able and devout men, as Prof. Milligan, Archdeacon Lee, Prof. Randell, Prof. Purves, and many others. The great teachers of the church have believed that while the stupendous symbolism is to be constantly recognized, the symbols themselves describe real events and actors. With them the Dragon is Satan, the Beast is the hostile power of the state, the harlot the apostate ecclesiastical system, and the heavenly Conqueror is Christ.

(2.) The book itself claims to be genuine prophecy. It fills, or seems to fill, the future with actual beings, some human, some extra-human, some Divine. But, if the spiritual explanation be true, then the book is an exaggeration and its pictures overdrawn and unnatural.

(3.) This theory ignores the plain statements of Revelation. Very distinctly and definitely the inspired writer furnishes certain chronological data that fix periods and events of the future which mark historical sequence and exact time-limits. In chap. xx: 2-7, six times the period of one thousand years is mentioned. It is the number from which we derive the idea of a Millennium. It is described as a period of blessedness, of Satan's imprisonment, of evil suppressed, of righteousness in the ascendency, of the universal sway of the heavenly Kingdom. That time is not put as ideal, as spiritual or figurative, but as actual and real. Other numbers are given, as *e. g.*, forty-two months, xi: 2; xiii: 5; twelve hundred and sixty days, xi: 3; xii: 6; time, times, and dividing of time, xii: 14—all which betoken history, reality.

(4.) Evil ever seeks to concentrate in a person or a system; so does good. Revelation shows us evil centralized in the Beast and in the False Prophet, and in their followers. Faithfulness and loyalty to God is also centralized in persons; in the two Witnesses, xi: in the angels who fill so large a place in the action of the book; in the Sun-clothed Woman and her Son; in the Palm-bearers, vii; and the Conqueror and His armies, xix. We cannot accept this method of explaining the book. For it empties it of much of its significance, and impeaches it as guilty of inflation and distortion. Whatever is true in it may be recognized, but as an interpretation it is wholly inadequate.

The third is, the *Historical Interpretation*. Briefly, it means this: the book is a prophetic history of the church and the world from the time of John to the final consummation at Christ's Advent. The predictions deal only with the most prominent events of this vast period, and not with details. The majority of Protestant commentators adopt it. Its dominant idea is this: the Seals, Trumpets and Vials are symbols of successive stages in the world's history. Each set belongs to a distinct class of events. So, likewise the explanatory visions, as chaps. x-xiv, mark epochs that follow each other in temporal sequence. Some of the ablest students of the book have sought to open these prophecies according to this principle, as Bengel,

Mead, Newton, Elliott, Guinness, and the late A. J. Gordon. That there is truth in this method of interpretation cannot be doubted by those who have made ecclesiastical and profane history a real study. The correspondence between the prediction and its historical fulfilment is too obvious and striking to be accidental or fortuitous. The one matches the other so marvellously that God is recognized as the author of the prophecy. It may at once be admitted that the prophecy is so constructed as to touch the salient events of our dispensation. But as a system of interpretation it is incomplete. It leaves huge gaps in the history of the past 1,800 years. A period of 500 years, from A. D. 1000 to 1500 inclusive, it leaves almost untouched. It rests chiefly on the year-day theory, i. e., that a day in prophetic Scripture stands for a year. This is extremely doubtful. Indeed, it does not now commend itself to sober interpreters as once it did. In the judgment of not a few, Tregelles has demonstrated it to be fallacious and unbiblical. But even assuming there is ground for it in the prophetic word, the historical expounders of Revelation are wide apart in its application. For instance, there is a number that frequently occurs in the book, viz.: 1,260 days, 42 months, three years and a half—the three denote the same period of time. A year for a day amounts to 1,260 years. The end of the 1,260 is the consummation of our age: it is the supreme crisis. But from what point is it to be dated? What is its *terminus a quo?* Here disagreement and divergence at once arise. Unanimity as to the starting-point of the 1,260

years there is none. Joachim (c. 1200) begins with
A. D. 1 and ends with A. D. 1260; Melancthon, A. D.
660-2000; Bengel, 576-1836; Mede, 455-1715; Flem-
ing, 606-1848; Gill, 606-1866; Elliott, 608-1868; Cun-
ningham, 533-1792; Fysh, 727-1987; Guinness, 672-
1932.

The fourth is the *Futurist*, which holds that the
predictions, particularly from chap. iv to chap. xx:
6, have their fulfilment in a brief space of time at the
close of our dispensation—the whole being limited to
some seven years, which end with the Lord's Advent.
With much of this view the writer agrees, not with all
of it. This will appear as we proceed with the ex-
amination of the various parts of the book.

CHAPTER IV.

PLAN AND STRUCTURE.

V. The Plan of the Revelation. Its structure is most artistic, unequalled in this respect, perhaps, by any other book of the Bible. To the superficial reader it presents a different appearance. To him it appears complex, confused, enigmatical, even unintelligible. It was on account of this popular notion of the book (in itself totally false) that Dr. South made his profane remark that has done no small injury—" that mysterious, extraordinary . . . book called the Revelation . . . which the more it is studied the less it is understood, as generally finding a man cracked or making him so." To the devout and patient student, who seeks to know the Lord's mind in all His word, it has no such character as South ascribes to it. He may not be able to grasp its full meaning, he may have to leave great tracts in it wholly unexplored because he cannot penetrate them, but he finds exquisite beauty in its structure, divine wisdom and infinite skill in the correlation and the combination of its various scenes and visions. Throughout a mighty plan runs. Order rules. God's purposes are disclosed. The book is an Apocalypse, not an enigma nor a puzzle.

First, note its use of numbers. This is remarkable both for frequency and peculiarity. We might truly say that Revelation has a numerical structure. Its

27

form to some considerable extent is governed by numbers.

(1.) *Three.* It is very prominent, nor is it confined to the idea of Trinity. It embraces more than individual completeness; it moulds sentences and paragraphs; it describes unseen and eternal realities. In i: 4, 5, 6, are three sets of three: we have " him who is, and who was, and who is to come;" Jesus Christ, " the faithful witness, the firstborn of the dead, the ruler of the kings of the earth;" believers are " loved, loosed from their sins, and made kings and priests unto God." John himself seems to assign a threefold division to this book, i: 19. " Write, therefore, the things which thou sawest, and the things which are, and the things which shall come to pass hereafter." The prominence given the number three in the fourth chapter is remarkable. In iv: 1 there is the door opened, the voice that summons John on high, and the promise. The nameless Occupant of the heavenly throne is like a jaspér, and a sardius gem, and the emerald-like rainbow encircles the throne, iv: 2. Three things distinguish the twenty-four elders; they are enthroned, are arrayed in white raiment, and are gold-crowned, iv: 4. Out of the throne proceed lightnings, and voices, and thunder, iv: 5. Before the throne, and round about it, and within it are three objects, viz.: seven lamps, a glassy sea, and four living creatures, iv: 5, 6. The four living creatures chant the Trisagion, " Holy, Holy, Holy "—addressed to " the Almighty who was and who is, and who is to come;" and they give Him " glory, and honor, and thanks," iv: 8, 9. The gold-crowned Elders, like-wise, in their magnificent chant give Him " glory, and honor, and power," iv: 11. Moreover, there are three Woe Trumpets, viii: 13; three frog-like spirits issue from the mouth of the dragon, from the mouth of the beast, and from the mouth of the false prophet, xvi: 13. In chap. xviii: 8, three plagues come upon Babylon—death, mourning and famine; and in the same chapter three classes of men wail over Babylon's Fall, Kings, ver. 9; merchants, ver. 11; seamen, ver. 17. These are but specimens of the significant use of this number *three*.

(2.) *Four*. By some this is supposed to be the number of creation. It certainly is found often in connection with earth and its forces. Chap. iv: 6-8 describes the four Living Creatures, which have four faces, viz.: the ox, the lion, the eagle, and man. They are the four great heads of creation, and they are most intimately associated with the Throne, iv: 6 (cf. Ezek. i: 5-28; x). Mention is made of the four corners of the earth, of the four angels stationed thereat, holding the four winds in their grasp, vii: 1; four angels, likewise, are stationed at the river Euphrates, their watch and their action are for a four-fold division of time, an hour, and a day, and a month, and a year, ix: 14, 15. In the awful carnage of the trodden Winepress, the blood of the slain extends for 1,600 furlongs, *i. e.*, the square of four multiplied by 100. In the first four Seals, four horses go forth at the call of the four living creatures, vi: 1-7. More-over, four often enters into the structure of sentences;

as, *e. g.,* v: 9; viii: 5; x: 11; xvi: 18; xviii: 22, etc.
In xxi: 8 there are eight descriptive epithets employed
touching the wicked, two sets of four, or four sets of
two.

In the messages to the Seven Churches there is a
division of them into two groups of three and four
respectively. In the first three, viz.: Ephesus, Smyrna,
and Pergamos, the exhortation to hear what the Spirit
says precedes the promise to the overcomer, ii: 7, 11,
17. But in the four that follow, viz.: Thyatira, Sardis, Philadelphia, and Laodicea, the exhortation to
hear what the Spirit says comes after the promise to
the overcomer, ii: 26-29; iii: 5, 6; iii: 12, 13; iii: 21, 22.
This is a remarkable combination of the numbers three
and four. Its significance is difficult to determine with
any satisfaction. These also are but specimens of the
use of four.

(3.) *Seven.* This number is not only employed to denote so many individual objects, but it enters very
largely into the whole plan of the book. Seven is the
number of completeness, of perfection, and of dispensa-
tional fulness. All readers know that there are four sets
of sevens that cover a very considerable section of the
book. These are the seven messages to the seven
churches, ii, iii. The vision of the seven seals, which
embraces v-viii: 1 (with an episode between the sixth
and the seventh of the series, viz.: vii). The vision
of the seven trumpets, viii: 2-xi: 16 (with an episode
between the sixth and the seventh, x-xi: 13). The
vision of the seven vails, xv: 5-xvi. Thus nearly one-
half of the book belongs to this fourfold series.

There are fourteen (a double seven) Songs or
Choruses in the Revelation, which the American Re-
vision rightly indicates by printing them on the page
as if they were poetry or quotations; which in fact
they are. These Songs are found through the book in
the following chapters: iv: 8, 11; v: 9, 12, 13; vii: 10,
12; xi: 15, 17, 18; xii: 10-12; xv: 3, 4; xix: 1, 2, 5, 6-8.

These Songs or rhythmical utterances are all spoken
by heavenly beings and in heaven, with one sole exception, *i. e.,* chap. v: 13, in which every created thing
in heaven, on earth, and under the earth breaks out in
tuneful ascription of praise and honor and blessing to
the Lamb, because He is now at length about to
redeem by power His vast inheritance, even as He has
once for all redeemed it by blood. It is gloriously
right and fitting that all creation should lift up its
voice in a majestic anthem of praise, since its time of
deliverance is finally come.

This, notable as it is, does not exhaust the use of
this number. It enters into passages where no direct
mention of it is made. Thus, in v: 12, seven attributes
of praise are ascribed to the Lamb that was slain; the
white-robed company in vii: 12 worship God with the
like number of ascriptions. Chap. xiv: 1-20 consists of
seven parts, viz.: the Lamb with His glorious company on mount Zion: the everlasting gospel: Babylon's
fall: the solemn threat against any fellowship with
the Beast: happy lot of those who die in the Lord
from henceforth: the harvest: the vintage. Besides,
the chapter mentions six angels, and One like the
Son of Man. The place of honor is given the Son of

man—three angels are on each side of Him, and He is in the midst, presiding over the vast movements. The climax of the series is in the number four, where He sits on the white Cloud.

The "seven spirits before the throne" (i: 4) express the infinite perfection of the Holy Spirit. The "seven stars" in Christ's right hand (i: 16) denote the complete authority He has over the churches. The Lamb has "seven horns and seven eyes" (v: 6), which denote the almighty power, the supreme intelligence, and the perfect omniscience with which He is endowed.

This may suffice to indicate how deeply the number seven is woven into the structure of Revelation, and how it dominates it. It would hardly be going too far to assert that the book is built on the principle of the septinary.

(4.) *Ten* is the number of secular organization and of power. The Beast has ten horns, and on his horns, ten diadems (xiii: 1). These are symbols of power. Ten joined with seven signifies the perfection of satanic force and worldly dominion. The Beast with seven heads and ten horns is the embodiment of devilish energy, and of apostate, imperial supremacy.

(5.) *Twelve* is the number of final and eternal perfection and duration. The Celestial City, the New Jerusalem (xxi, xxii: 5), has twelve foundations, with twelve gates, with twelve angel sentinels and guardians; the City is a majestic cube, twelve thousand furlongs being the measure of its form. The tree of life yields twelve manner of fruits, and yields them through twelve months of a cycle.

Auberlin does not exaggerate this feature of the Apocalypse when he says, " The history of salvation is mysteriously governed by holy numbers. They are the scaffolding of the organic edifice. They are not merely outward indications of time, but indications of nature and essence. Scripture and antiquity put numbers as the fundamental forms of things where we put ideas."

A second significant phase of the structure of Revelation deserves careful scrutiny. It may be called the plan of *recapitulation,* or better, perhaps, *parallelism.* What is meant is this: the chief series of visions, *e. g.,* the Seals, Trumpets, and Vials, do not succeed each other in historical and chronological sequence, but move side by side. They do not all have the same starting-point, but they all arrive at the same goal; namely, the final consummation. They all lead up to the transcendant event which is the central theme of the book, the personal Advent of our Lord Jesus Christ. Victorinus, the earliest commentator on the Apocalypse, wrote: " The order of the things said is not to be regarded, since often the Holy Spirit when He has run to the end of the last time again returns to the same times and supplies what He has less fully expressed." His view is that of many modern expositors.

The same peculiarity of structure appears in the book of Daniel. In chap. ii of that book we have the four hostile World Monarchies represented by a huge metallic Image and its destruction by the Stone. In chap. vii, the same World-Power is symbolized by four predatory beasts. Chap. viii gives the prophetic history of two of these same Powers, and chaps. x, xi, xii, trace the action and the overthrow of the same great enemy. Like John, Daniel traces one line of prediction down to the consummation; then he returns to follow a second, then a third, and finally a fourth— all terminating at the End-time. It is prophetic recapitulation, apocalyptic parallelism. It is a style peculiar to these two books of the Bible. To ignore it, or to fail to recognize it as the fundamental phase of the book's structure, is to deprive the student of the true interpretation, and is sure to lead into all sorts of vagaries and speculations.

Proof of such parallelism of the great Vision above referred to is now to be submitted. James Smith calls the process " folding back," *i. e.,* each vision as it is introduced and described folds back upon the vision which precedes it. In other words, the process is that of contemporaneousness, and not that of succession at all, as so many interpreters of the book have thought.

It is very noteworthy that the Seals, Trumpets, and Vials, all alike end in mysterious " voices," and in cosmical convulsions and revolutions. (The introduction of the angel-trumpeters is before the effects of the opening of the seventh Seal are described, viii: 2; their beginning to sound is after the seventh Seal's effects are announced, viii: 3-5.) The opening of the seventh Seal is followed by " voices, and thunderings,

and lightnings, and an earthquake," viii: 5. The
seventh Trumpet is succeeded by "lightnings, and
voices, and thunderings, and an earthquake, and great
hail," xi: 19. The pouring out of the seventh Vial
is followed by "voices, and thunders, and lightnings;
and there was a great earthquake, such as was not since
men were upon the earth, so mighty an earthquake, and
so great," xvi: 18. It will be noted that these Voices
and Cosmic Convulsions occur under the seventh of
each group, and that they are identical in character,
and almost entirely identical in language. Unmistakably they point to the same event, they describe the
like tremendous phenomena, they belong to the same
world-wide catastrophe; namely, the final consummation, the End-time, when Jesus Christ shall again appear in majesty and glory in this our earth, and forever terminate the deadly struggle between His rule
and Satan's. It seems perfectly clear from the facts
just stated that these Visions are contemporaneous,
that they follow the same general course, that they
pertain to the same period of time, and that, therefore,
they are parallel with each other. They are synchron-
ous; not successive, with long intervals between.

Furthermore, the student of the Revelation cannot
fail to note the striking similarity, the almost exact
identity which subsists between the action of the
Trumpets and of the Vials. They belong to the same
sphere, they move in the same circle of events, and
cover the like field. The subjoined table confirms the
foregoing statement:

Trumpets.	Vials.
First. The earth, chap. viii: 7.	The earth, chap. xvi: 2.
Second. The sea, viii: 8.	The sea, xvi: 3.
Third. Rivers, fountains, viii: 10.	Rivers and fountains, xvi: 4.
Fourth. Sun, moon, stars, viii: 12.	The sun, xvi: 8.
Fifth. The abyss, king Abaddon, ix: 11.	Throne of the Beast, xvi: 10.
Sixth. River Euphrates, ix.	River Euphrates, xvi: 12.
Seventh. Voices, thunders, etc., xi: 15, 19.	Voices, thunders, etc., 17, 18.

A careful inspection of this table is enough to persuade us that these two groups of visions move along the same lines, although each has peculiarities that pertain to itself. They touch the same points, they begin, they progress, and they end precisely alike. The main difference between the two lies in the extent of their respective action; the Trumpets are restricted in their action; the Vials are universal. The Trumpets smite the third part of the earth, the third part of the sea, the third part of the rivers and fountains, and the third part of the sun. These four Trumpets are limited thus to a definite and partial area. The four Vials corresponding to these Trumpets are not so restricted, they blast the whole of that which they strike. In the first and second of the Woe Trumpets there is exemption for the grass and the trees, but unutterable judgment for the men who had not the seal of God in their foreheads, unutterable torment, likewise, for the third part of men. The fifth and sixth Vials are not confined to a particular sphere as are the Woe Trumpets; they desolate the Beast's throne, they strike his kingdom with judicial blindness, they marshal the whole apostate world for the final and overwhelming conflict, the battle of the great day of God the Almighty. The seventh Trumpet peals forth the glad news, "The Kingdom of the world is to become the Kingdom of our Lord and of his Christ: and he shall reign for ever and ever." The pouring out of the seventh Vial brings the " great voice out of the temple, from the throne, saying, It is done." Fairbairn is right when he says, " These two lines of symbolic representation . . . are alike in their commencement, their progress, and their termination." The Trumpets start with a limited infliction of the wrath of God upon the guilty rebels of the last days, but they deepen in sevenfold energy as they move on to the end. In like manner the Vials intensify in severity, for they are the " seven last plagues," and in them " the wrath of God is fulfilled."

Moreover, certain " catchwords," as Wordsworth calls them, bind the visions together, thus demonstrating the identity of the objects in view. Thus, the fellow-servants and brethren of the martyrs who were to be slain (vi: 9-11) connect with the blessed dead who die in the Lord (xiv: 12, 13), and with those who share in the first resurrection (xx: 6). The earthquake under the sixth Seal connects with the earthquake of the sixth Trumpet (vi: 12; xi: 13). Under the fifth Trumpet the ungodly seek death, and death flies from them (ix: 6). Under the fifth Vial men gnaw their tongues for pain and blaspheme God

(xvi: 10, 11). The Beast which first appears between
the sixth and the seventh Trumpets (xi: 7) connects
with the Beast of xiii and the Red Dragon of xii. The
sealing of 144,000 (vii: 1-8) connects with the same
number in chap. xiv: 1-5. The lamb-like Beast from
the earth speaks as a Dragon (xiii: 11). The word
Dragon occurs twelve times in the Revelation, and is
always applied to Satan. This earth-Beast, therefore,
that looks so lamb-like, is in reality satanic, for he is
the servant and tool of the Dragon (xii: 9). He is
the False Prophet. By such "catchwords" the various visions and parts of the book are knit together
in closest unity. The same peculiarity of structure is
seen in the various "episodes" and intercalary visions.
Thus, the episode of the "Sealed and the Saved,"
vii: 1-17, is placed between the sixth and the seventh
Seals. The episode relating to the angel with the
little book and the two witnesses is inserted between
the sixth and seventh Trumpet, x, xi: 1-14. The
episode of the gathering of the world's army for the
final and decisive battle is placed between the sixth
and seventh Vial, xvi: 13-16. All this, and much
might be added to it, displays how the Seer has riveted
together his matchless book into a perfect unity of
parts and of contents.

John even ties up his predictions with those of
Daniel, as the four wild Beasts of Daniel (Dan. vii)
appear also in the Apocalypse (xiii: 2).

Once more: in addition to the episodes, there are
intercalated visions in the progress of the Revelation,
which are essential parts of its structure, and which ad-

vance its central idea, the coming of the Lord and the establishment of His Kingdom in victory over the whole earth. These are, the Sun-clothed Woman and the Dragon (xii) ; the Beast and the False Prophet (xiii) ; the mighty program of the End-time (xiv) ; Babylon, the Beast, and Babylon's Doom (xvii, xviii, xix: 10). It is to be noted that Chaps. xii-xiv are interposed between the Trumpet and the Vial Visions; that chaps. xvii-xix: 10 are interposed between the Vial judgments and the actual, visible Advent, judgment, and first resurrection described in xix: 11-xx: 6. A large part of the book is thus made up of the episodes and intercalated visions, and they are all explanatory and interpretative. Without them, how much more enigmatical and difficult the book would be, and how immense the chasm would be in it if these were dropped out.

The Revelation encloses visions within visions, and scenes within scenes. The query may arise, Can any explanation be made of this peculiar plan of the book —this involved and complex structure? None; save that it pleased the Lord so to construct it; and this should satisfy the believer. Two advantages to us, however, seem to be derived from this divine method of revelation. One is this: it serves to display in the most graphic manner the vastness of the field which the book covers. Beyond all doubt the Revealer deals with the world's crisis, with the consummation of all God's ways with the earth, with the time when the " mystery of God shall be finished " (x: 7). Heaven, earth, and hell will then engage in a struggle such as our planet has never known before, and probably will never again know.   The issue will be eternal victory. So far as we in our profound ignorance may perceive, the sublime symbolism of the book could alone set forth adequately the magnitude of the " battle of the great day of God, the Almighty."   Another is : the plan affords the introduction of circumstantial details, and minute descriptions of the forces and influences that will come into collision at the time of the End.   After the Seer has traced one line of prediction down to the crisis and climax, he returns and starts afresh with another, going over the same road, but presenting other phases and aspects of the same awful period.   This he does again and again, for one set of symbols cannot tell all he has to communicate ; he must add, expand, interject before he has done. Other features more dreadful than any yet sketched must be shown ; deeper and darker shades must be put in, more lurid and appalling colors must be laid on, before the stupendous picture is complete.   Each vision in turn contributes an essential part to the whole, and the whole reveals the character and the scenes of the last days with a fulness and distinctness of outline and detail such as could not be presented by any other plan.

CHAPTER V.

ANALYSIS—THREE FORMS.

VI. Analysis. Three forms are submitted. The first is the partition of the contents under heads and particulars as these are marked in the book itself. It rests on the plan and structure of Part V.

The second is a tabular exhibition of the contents, following, mainly, the outlines constructed by Principal Randell, and by the late Dr. Nathaniel West.

The third furnishes still another partition of the contents, and this is copied from the very suggestive "Analysis of the Apocalypse," by Dr. W. J. Erdman.

It is fondly hoped that the three will serve to open to the reader this profound and difficult book, as, perhaps, he may not have seen nor understood it hitherto. Certain it is, the three studied together, as well as separately, will tend to lead him into a larger knowledge of the book, and a more distinct and definite view of its contents, than perhaps he might not otherwise receive.

FIRST.

A. Prologue, chap. i: 1-8

B. Vision of the Glorified Son of Man, i: 9-20.

C. Epistles to the Seven Churches, ii, iii.

D. Vision of Heaven, introductory, iv-v.
    The Throne, The Elders, Living Beings, Sealed
    Book and the Lamb.

E. Opening of the Seven Seals, vi-viii: 1.
    First Four Seals, vi: 1-8, Fifth, Martyrs, vi: 9-11.
    Sixth, supernatural signs, vi: 12-17; Seventh,
    viii: 1, 5.
    Episode: (a) Sealing 144,000 of Israel, vii: 1-8.
    　　　　　(b) Innumerable company of Saved
    　　　　　　　Gentiles, vii: 9-17.

F. Sounding of Seven Trumpets, viii: 7-xi: 19.
    First Four Trumpets, viii: 7-12; Three Woe
    Trumpets, viii: 13-xi: 19.
    Episode: (a) Angel and Little Book, x.
    　　　　　(b) Temple and Two Witnesses, xi:
    　　　　　　　1-14

G. Visions Interposed between Trumpets and Vials,
    chaps. xii-xiv.
    Sun-clothed Woman and Dragon, xii.
    Beast from the Sea, xiii: 1-10.
    Beast from the Earth, xiii: 11-18.
    Lamb and His Company on Mt. Zion, xiv: 1-5.
    Four Great Proclamations, xiv: 6-13.
    The Harvest, xiv: 14-16.
    The Vintage, xiv: 17-20.

H. Vision of the Seven Vials, xv, xvi.
    Song of Victors at Glassy Sea, xv: 1-4.
    Prelude to Judgments, xv: 5-8.

The Seven Judgments, xvi.
Episode, **xvi**: 13-16, armies afield.

I. Visions Interposed between Vials and Actual Advent, xvii-xix: 10.
Harlot and Beast, xvii.
Doom, xviii.
Joyous Hallelujahs, xix: 1-10.

J. Visible Advent of the Lord Jesus Christ, chaps. xix: 11-xx: 6.
The Epiphany, xix: 11-18.
Doom of Beast and False Prophet, xix: 19-21.
Satan's Imprisonment, xx: 1-3.
Resurrection and Millennium, xx: 4-6.

K. Final Revolt and Final Judgment, xx: 7-15.

L. City of God, xxi-xxii: 5.

M. Epilogue, xxii: 6-21.

SECOND.

The Christophany: Vision of the glorified Son of Man, chapter i: 1–20.	Consummation: Advent of Christ.

The Seven Churches, chaps. ii, iii.

The En of the Age.

(1)	(2)	(3)	(4)	(5)	(6)	(7)
Ephesus:	Smyrna:	Pergamos:	Thyatira:	Sardis:	Philadelphia:	Laodicea:
Chap. ii: 1-7.	ii: 8-11.	ii: 12-17.	ii: 18-29.	iii: 1-6.	iii: 7-13.	iii: 14-22.

The Vision of Heaven, chaps. iv, v.

The Throne, Seven Lamps of Fire, 24 Elders, 4 Living Creatures, Angels, Book, Lamb.

The Seven Seals, chaps. vi, vii, viii: 1–5.

The End.

1 Seal.	2 Seal.	3 Seal.	4 Seal.	5 Seal.	6 Seal.		7 Seal.
White Horse,	Red Horse,	Black Horse,	Pale Horse,	Martyrs,	Signs	⌈Episode⌉	
vi: 1, 2.	vi: 3, 4.	vi: 5, 6.	vi: 7, 8.	vi: 9-11.	vi: 12-17.	⌊ vii— ⌋	viii: 1-5.

The Seven Trumpets, chaps. viii: 6–xi.

The End.

1st	2d	3d	4th	5th	6th	⌈Episode⌉	7th
viii: 7.	viii: 8, 9.	viii: 10, 11.	viii: 12, 13.	ix: 1-12.	ix: 13-21.	⌊x, xi: 14⌋	xi: 15-19.

Interposed Visions, explanatory and interpretive, chaps. xii–xiv.

The End

Sign in Heaven, xii Sun-clothed Woman and Great Red Dragon.	Beasts from Sea and Earth, xiii.	Program of Events, xiv. Harvest and Vintage.

The Seven Vials, chaps. xv, xvi.
Last Plagues.

The End.

1st	2d	3d	4th	5th	6th	⌈ Episode ⌉	7th
xvi: 2.	xvi: 3.	xvi: 4-7.	xvi: 8, 9.	xvi: 10, 11.	xvi: 12.	⌊xvi: 13-16.⌋	xvi: 17-21.

Interposed Explanatory Visions, chaps. xvii–xix: 1–10.

The End.

The Harlot Babylon and Beast, xvii.	Doom, xviii, xix: 1-5.	Marriage of Lamb, xix: 6-10.

Visions of Epiphany of Christ: Beasts and armies overwhelmed—Resurrection of Saints, chaps. xix: 11–xx: 6.	The End. Millennium.
Vision of the Last Revolt and the Last Judgment, chap. xx: 7–15.	Absolute End.
Vision of the City of God—Paradise Restored, chaps. xxi, xxii.	Eternity.

THIRD.

An Analysis of the Apocalypse.
[W. J. ERDMAN, D.D.]

I THE SEVEN CHURCHES

1: 1-8	The Prologue	
1: 9-20	The Son of Man	
2: 1-3: 22	The Seven Churches	

II THE SEVEN SEALS

4: 1-5: 14	Introduction	The Throne, the Lamb and the Book
6: 1-17	Progression	The Six Seals
7: 1-17	Episode	The Sealed and the Saved
8: 1	Consummation	The Seventh Seal

III THE SEVEN TRUMPETS

8: 2-5	Introduction	The Angel and the Incense
8: 6-9: 21	Progression	The Six Trumpets
10: 1-11: 14	Episode	The Angel, the little Book, the Two Witnesses
11: 15-19	Consummation	The Seventh Trumpet

IV THE SEVEN PERSONAGES

12: 1-13: 1 a	Introduction	The Two Signs in Heaven
13: 1 b-18	Progression	The Great Tribulation
14: 1-13	Episode	The First Fruits and the Three Angels
14: 14-20	Consummation	The Harvest and the Vintage

V THE SEVEN VIALS

15: 1-8	Introduction	The Overcomers and the Seven Angels
16: 1-12	Progression	The Six Vials
16: 13-16	Episode	The Gathering of the Kings
16: 17-21	Consummation	The Seventh Vial

VI THE SEVEN DOOMS

17: 1-18	Introduction	The Babylon and the Beast
18: 1-24	Progression	The Doom of Babylon
19: 1-10	Episode	The Four Hallels
19: 11-20: 15	Consummation	The Six Final Dooms

VII THE SEVEN NEW THINGS

21: 1-8	Introduction	New Heaven, Earth, Peoples
21: 9-22: 5	The New Jerusalem	City, Temple
22: 6-21	The Epilogue	Luminary, Paradise

CHAPTER VI.

They **are** inscribed thus: "John to the seven churches which are in Asia (i: 4). Asia, of course, does not mean the Continent, nor even Asia Minor, but the Province of Asia in Western Asia Minor. The Seven Churches were contiguous to each other, the greatest distance between any two of them being some fifty miles, while in the case of some, *e. g.*, Thyatira, Sardis and Philadelphia, hardly twenty miles lay between. Other groups of Christians besides those named were found in the same territory even in Paul's time (A. D. 62-3), as at Colossae and Hierapolis (Col. iv: 13). Ignatius (c. A. D. 110, *i. e.*, less than twenty years after John wrote the book) addressed letters to prosperous churches at Tralles and Magnesia in the same region, and it is presumable they existed when the Revelation was sent forth. Philip the Evangelist and his daughters, who entertained Paul in their home at Cæsarea (Acts xxi: 8, 9), afterwards removed to Hierapolis, where Polycarp, disciple of John **and** pastor at Smyrna, saw the daughters, and no doubt talked with them of the great Apostle (Prof. Gregory). Near this same period (c. A. D. 120-30) Papias, who perhaps saw and heard John himself, became the chief pastor at Hierapolis. All these

46

various churches, Colossae, Hierapolis, Tralles, Magnesia, and others far more widely known and influential flourished at the close of the first century. Now, how happens it that these assemblies, so prominent and important, are passed by in total silence in the book, while those of which we know little or nothing, except in the case of two, beyond what is told us in chaps. ii, iii, hold so conspicuous a place in the Lord's messages? Why are these seven singled out and addressed, and all the rest of the whole world ignored? The only reasonable explanation is this: These seven here addressed contained in themselves the characteristic features of the entire church in John's day, while the others did not. Accordingly, far more than local and historical interest attaches to them. These Seven embraced in their conditions, in their circumstances and in their tendencies the prophetic history of the entire Christian Body from John down to the final consummation at the coming of the Lord Jesus Christ. That is, the seven churches and the messages addressed to them represent the whole church of John's time, and they likewise sketch in broad outlines its history to the end.

This conclusion is warranted by the following considerations: (1) The divine command to the Seer was to write out and send the whole Apocalypse to these churches: "What thou seest, write in a book, and send it to the seven churches," i: 11. Certainly the Revelation was not intended for these Christian assemblies alone, but for all the people of God throughout the earth. (2) The book is one of symbols from the first chapter to the last, and if chaps. **ii, iii,** form an exception, they constitute an unaccountable anomaly. (3) The term "mystery"—"the mystery of the seven stars . . . and of the seven golden candlesticks" (i: 20)—points to the hidden meaning of the symbols, "the sacred secret signified by them" (Lyra). (4) The mystic use of the number *seven* throughout the book that in every instance denotes completeness, perfection, clearly indicates the symbolic character of these chapters. (5) The contents of the messages contemplate the whole church and its entire history, as the repeated announcement of Christ's coming proves, ii: 16, 25; iii: 3, 11. (6) The appeal to "hear what the Spirit saith to the churches" attests the same truth, the language includes the whole body (cf. i: 19, 20; iv: 1; xxii: 6, 16). Not a single church is exhorted, but all "the churches."

Each of the seven had marked peculiarities and characteristic features that cannot be restricted to one local assembly, for they foreshadow the like state in the church universal to the close of the dispensation. A study of their moral condition, however brief and cursory, will serve to show that their excellencies and their defects so faithfully and unsparingly pointed out by the glorified Lord cannot be applied exclusively to the close of the apostolic age. They have reproduced themselves in the professing body in all the subsequent centuries down to the present day.

The "angel" of Ephesus (*i. e.,* Christ's messenger

and representative, certainly not a heavenly being nor a Diocesan Bishop who had no existence in the first century, but the responsible pastor), is both praised and censured. The praise is cordial, and the censure tender but unsparing. Ephesus was the mother of the Asian churches, and the titles our Lord here takes describe His supreme authority and His abiding presence. This assembly was zealous in every good work, steadfast in its testimony, patient under trial, intolerant of false teachers; but she had declined from her first love, she had " fallen." Will any deny that the like condition is exhibited in evangelical bodies of the present time? Zeal, activity in service and works of all sorts predominate; but is love for Christ, the longing to see Him, to be with Him, to be filled with His loving presence what it once was or should be?

Smyrna (ii: 8-11) is the martyr church, and represents suffering. " Tribulation for ten days " may foreshadow the persecutions under the Roman Empire, but must not be confined to that period. Smyrna prefigures the suffering the people of God endure through their entire history. The Lord's titles here, as in every message, are exactly adapted to the state of the church. He is the first and the last, who was dead and is alive again; and His servants who suffer and die for His name shall also live again.

A serious condition is found at Pergamum, ii: 12-17. She dwells where " Satan's throne is." At Pergamum Satan was enthroned and held his court. The reference is, probably, to the new Cæsar-worship which was fast spreading over the Roman world. It

4

was pre-eminent at Pergamum (Profs. Ramsay, Swete). The fanatical and jealous Domitian exerted his vast power to advance the absurd cult, and he sought by wily schemes to have himself worshipped as a god! The insidious plea was: "What evil is there in saying, 'Lord Cæsar,' or burning a few grains of incense before his statue?" But this would be idolatrous, would be to "commit fornication," and to deny Christ! There were those there who taught this vile doctrine—"the teaching of Balaam," who taught Balak to allure Israel to their ruin when he could not obtain the Lord's permission to curse them. Alliance with the world is chiefly meant. The roaring lion is exchanged for the serpent, the adversary for the deceiver. Persecution, painful as it is, is not so perilous as worldly alliance. When Constantine recognized Christianity, when he sat in the Council of Nicea as an adviser, the fatal way to union of church and state began to be prepared. Pergamum thus becomes a prophetic symbol of the Christian Body in its lamentable connection with the godless World-power.

A more subtle danger appears in Thyatira, ii: 18-29. The virus in this church is the crafty teaching of the Woman Jezebel. She calls herself a prophetess, she seduces and corrupts the new people of God as Ahab's heathen wife did both her husband and Israel. It is not necessary we should understand that a veritable woman lived and wrought her evil in Thyatira, although the reading, "thy wife Jezebel," is well supported, and is very suggestive. The language is symbolical; the meaning of the symbol is unmistakable; it points to a wicked influence, seductive, secret, powerful, that, if unchecked, would subvert the whole testimony of the church and lead these converted heathen straight back into idolatry with all its impure practices. Thyatira typically with this prophetess teaching and debasing and corrupting is the Lord's adumbration of the rise and reign of Popery, a system idolatrous and persecuting, Jezebel-like, practicing its wickedness under a religious disguise.

A faithful remnant in Thyatira is recognized and separated from the mass of the professing body— "But to you I say, to the rest," ver. 24. They are the historical types of those Christians who through the centuries stood aloof from unfaithful Christendom and who worshipped God in spirit and truth.

All this evinces the predictive character of the Seven Messages and Churches.

But may not these Seven Churches mark off prophetically seven periods or stages in the church's history from the Apostles to the end of the dispensation? So many think, from Joseph Mede and Sir Isaac Newton to the present time. There is harmony among these writers as to the fact of such periods, there is not as to the exact periods covered by them. Perhaps the nearest to uniformity is found in the following temporal partition: Ephesus prefigures the apostolic age closing with the first century: Smyrna, the age of the persecutions, the martyr time from A. D. 100 to A. D. 325: Pergamos, church and state united, to the middle of the eighth century: Thyatira, the Middle Ages: Sardis, the times succeeding the Reformation, from the close of the sixteenth century to the latter half of the eighteenth: Philadelphia, to about our own time: Laodicea, the last period when rejection and judgment take place and the End arrives. The Laodicean stage is still future, though there are unmistakable symptoms and premonitions that it has almost arrived.

The above distribution is not altogether satisfactory, for it is not historically accurate. For example, Smyrna undoubtedly marks the period of martyrdom, but two of the most virulent and frightful persecutions which the Church has ever suffered occurred in the first century, under Nero and Domitian. And long after Constantine and the so-called conversion of the Roman Empire to Christianity, uncounted multitudes of the purest and the best of God's servants on earth went to the stake or were slain by the sword during the Middle Ages and every century since. Smyrna cannot rightly be confined to the time between A. D. 100-325.

No more can Sardis (iii: 1-6) be restricted to post-Reformation times, as some would fain have us believe. For while a dead formalism pervaded Christendom in the 17th and 18th centuries, it was by no means universal, as the Pietists of Germany, the Huguenots of France, and the Puritans of Britain attest. "Thou hast a name that thou livest, and art dead" describes far more closely the dark period lying between the Pontifical savages and pagans, Popes Innocent III and Leo X—a period of some three centuries. In the hundred years preceding the

Reformation (A. D. 1410-1510) the Roman See sank down to the lowest point in infamy that it has ever reached. Four Popes, " each worse than the others " (as Italians say), by their loathsome characters and their foul deeds, stamped that century with eternal disgrace. They were known as John XXIII, Sixtus IV, Innocent VIII, and Alexander VI. It was the deplorable state into which the church had fallen that made the Reformation a necessity if Christianity were to survive. No interpretation of the Seven Churches which contradicts church history can be right. The Sardis condition belongs to pre-Reformation times rather than to any stage in the history of Protestantism. The Seven Churches do mark stages of history, but often they overlap, two or more of them covering the same period. Indeed, they are mirrors in which the condition of the universal church may see itself reflected at any stage of its existence.

The characteristics of the church of Philadelphia distinguish our day—so some rashly assert. It is a joy to know that there are multitudes of Christians whose fidelity, devotion and hope for the Lord's speedy coming entitle them to rank as saints of the Philadelphian type. But side by side with these are other multitudes, called Christians, who exhibit the worst features found in Pergamum, in Thyatira, in Sardis, and in Laodicea. Let us not be blinded either by a false optimism or a stupid pessimism. We believe that all the phases of these seven assemblies of Asia co-exist in our day. The last two of the Seven, viz.: Philadelphia and Laodicea, demand a more extended study than can here be given them. Some remarks, however, touching them are submitted, for it is believed that misapprehension of the Lord's messages to them largely prevails.

Philadelphia. Christ promises to keep those who keep the word of His patience (iii: 10). The promise is to keep them from the "hour (season) of temptation (trial), that *hour* which is to come upon the whole world, to try (tempt) them that dwell upon the earth," iii: 10. Noteworthy is the term "trial," or "temptation." It is not named *the tribulation* so often mentioned in prophetic Scripture (vii: 14; Matt. xxiv: 21; Mark xiii: 19, etc.), but *trial*. No doubt it is closely associated with the Great Tribulation, but the word here used seems deliberately chosen, and points to the frightful dangers and temptations to which God's people will be exposed at the time of the End. We know from Rev. xiii: 13-15, 2 Thess. ii: 9-12, that portentous "signs" and lying "wonders" and the "deceit of unrighteousness," wrought by the Beast and the False Prophet, will daze and fascinate vast throngs of men, nay, we are told the world itself will "wonder after the beast," and "worship" him. There will be believers who must face that tremendous peril. This will be their trial—deny God, or die. It is the troublous time which immediately precedes the Advent. Hence Christ adds, "I come quickly." It is the End-time, the close of the Church period and of the dispensation.

But how will he keep these saints from the hour of trial? Many excellent students of the Revelation answer, By taking them away from earth into heaven. Accordingly, they find here in this promise the "rapture" of 1 Thess. iv: 16, 17. In such case these saints do not go into the trial at all, the rapture antedates the trial by some short space of time, some say seven years, others make it longer. It would be a blessed thing if this view could be substantiated, but it cannot. The language of the promise itself is fatal to it: "I will keep thee from the hour of temptation which cometh," etc. The natural and obvious meaning is, the safekeeping of them in the midst of worldwide trial, not exemption from it by being caught up to heaven. The preposition "out of" (*ek*) signifies exactly this, and not rapture before the trial begins. In all John's writings there is but one parallel passage with this: Jno. xvii: 15, "I pray not that thou shouldest take them out of the world, but that thou shouldest keep them from the evil." "Keep them from the evil" is identical in structure with "keep them from the hour of trial." None can possibly mistake what the Lord meant in His prayer: His disciples were to remain in the world, but He asks that they be kept from its evil, or from the evil one who is its god. So precisely in Rev. iii: 10, Philadelphian saints are to be in the trial, but safeguarded therein. This explanation is confirmed by the words that follow: "Behold I come quickly: hold fast that which thou hast, that no one take thy crown." Christ lays upon them the responsibility of vigilance, of continual effort. Each church, Philadelphia no less than the others, is called to guard its own inheritance, lest through unfaithfulness or apathy it lose its **crown**. The solemn exhortation involves the fact of trial and of danger. Philadelphia is to be in the trial, but kept safely in it, not raptured away before the trial begins.

Laodicea. This is the last stage and the worst of all, the most hopeless. Christ stands here without, as if shut out of His own house, a stranger who knocks at His own door for admittance. He intimates that the condition now reached has become intolerable, nauseating; rejection and judgment are held back only so long as He waits and knocks. Obviously when this deplorable state is reached the " falling away " (apostasy) of 2 Thess. ii: 3 is at the flood; the world is ripe for the *parousia* of the Man of Sin and the day of Christ.

There is some resemblance between this Laodicea condition and " Babylon," the great Harlot of chaps. xvii, xviii. Laodicea boasts of her wealth and her self-sufficiency, totally oblivious of her true state as wretched, poor, blind and naked (iii: 17). The Harlot's proud boast is, " I sit a queen, and am no widow, and shall see no sorrow." She is decked with gold, precious stones, with purple and scarlet (xviii: 7, 16), rich and contented as Laodicea. The Lord's call, " Come out of her, my people, that ye be not partakers of her sins, and that ye receive not of her plagues " (xviii: 4), is much like that to Laodicea, " Behold, I stand at the door and knock: if any man hear my voice and open the door, I will come into him, and sup with him, and he with me " (iii: 20). There are saints in Babylon, and in Laodicea likewise. The whole attitude of the Saviour before this Seventh Church indicates that He has people in it, that these His people must be separated from the corrupt and apostate company before His judgment falls. And the same thing happens precisely with those associated with Babylon. These, too, are called out before the wrath falls on the guilty apostates. Further on in this study we shall see that there are martyrs in the Great Tribulation, and there are those who are kept safely in it, as *e. g.,* 144,000 sealed ones (Rev. vii: 1-8), and the believers of Philadelphia (iii: 7-12). They are in the trial, but are safely guarded in it.

The conclusion is: The Seven Churches and the Messages addressed to them cover the whole church period, from the writing of the Apocalypse down to the final consummation, the Coming of the Lord. The three great septinary visions of the Seals, Trumpets and Vials also terminate in the final consummation. Each of them ends with the signal event of the book, the Coming of the Lord. But the difference between these four sets of sevens is very marked, and briefly is this: the Seven Churches embrace in their typical characteristics the entire dispensation lying between the apostolic age and the Second Advent. The visions of the Seals, Trumpets and Vials relate, in their full accomplishment, to the events which shall signalize the closing scenes of the age. These latter gather into a comparatively brief period of time just before Christ comes.

CHAPTER VII.

THE VISION OF HEAVEN OPENED, chaps. iv, v.

"After these things I saw, and behold a door opened in heaven," iv: 1, R. V. The phrase, "after these things," denotes apparently the transition from one vision to another (vii: 1, 9; xv: 5; xviii: 1; xix: 1). Even i: 19, held by many to be the division of the book, probably means the past, present and future as to visions, not the past, present and future of history, for much of chaps ii, iii relates to the future of the churches, not to the present alone. The phrase marks the succession of the visions and not of time. The last clause of iv: 1, "things which must be hereafter," is explained by Dan. ii: 28, 45. The visions of chaps. iv-vii: 1 appear to be denoted by it. (The Greek text of W. & H. and the margins of Eng. and Amer. revisions punctuate thus: "come to pass. After these things straightway," etc., which yields excellent sense.)

Grouped round about the resplendent central Throne, the Seer beheld four and twenty other thrones, lower, no doubt, upon which were seated four and twenty Elders clothed in white raiment, and on their heads crowns of gold. It is by no means easy to determine who, or what these Elders are. The majority of writers think they represent the redeemed of the Old and the New Testament epochs, twelve symbolizing one section, twelve the other of our race. There are some who believe they may be princely leaders of the heavenly hosts of unfallen spirits in heavenly worship (Craven in Lange). The language employed respecting them, the language they themselves employ is quite remarkable. The text of Revelation agreed upon by the English and American Revisers, and the latest critical Greek text of Westcott and Hort, of Weymouth and Nestle (not to mention others), presents a significant divergence from that of King James. In the revised version of v: 9, we are bidden read thus: "Worthy art thou to take the book, and to open the seals thereof; for thou wast slain, and didst purchase unto God with thy blood *men* of every tribe, and tongue, and people, and nation, and madest them *to be* unto our God a kingdom and priests; and they reign upon the earth." This was the "new song" sung by the Elders and the four living beings to the Lamb. They do not associate themselves with saved men in this hymn of praise; they actually appear to place themselves apart from the redeemed. In chap. vii: 9, 10, the unnumbered throng of the redeemed from among men sing their glad hossanah, "Salvation unto our God which sitteth on the throne, and unto the Lamb." But the Elders, and angels, and living beings do not join in it, they sing a different song from this of the saved. Moreover, one of the Elders said to John, "These which are arrayed in the white robes, who are they, and whence came they?" He himself explains, vii: 13-15; but this explanation seems to set a wide distinction between himself and the white-robed company. Indeed, in every passage where the voice of the Elders and of the four living beings is heard, they are not united with the redeemed (iv: 11; v: 12, xi: 17; xix: 4). The Elders are enthroned and crowned, but the souls of the martyrs—certainly the noblest portion of the redeemed—are seen beneath the altar, vi: 9-11, as if they were still in the state of martyrdom, their blood being at the altar's bottom like that of sacrificial victims. They are disembodied spirits, they have had as yet no resurrection nor reward. Accordingly, the Elders cannot be the totality of the redeemed already raised up and glorified, for here are saints still in the disembodied state, who are distinct from the Elders, and who are unglorified. And other martyrs are to follow these, vi: 11.

The best explanation of the vision of the Elders we have seen is by Dr. Swete, in his very recent commentary on the Apocalypse (1906-7), and it is embodied in this sentence: " The twenty-four Elders are the Church in its totality, but the Church idealized and, therefore, seen as already clad in white, crowned, and enthroned in the Divine Presence—a state yet future (*must be hereafter*), but already potentially realized in the resurrection and ascension of the Head, cf. Eph. ii: 6."

The four living creatures, iv: 6-8. " Beasts " of A. V. is most unfortunate as a translation, for these beings are neither brutes nor wild beasts like the two described in chap. xiii. These are distinguished for their vitality, their intense livingness, as their name (*zoa*) indicates, for their activity in the worship and service of God, and for their composite appearance.

They have the faces and forms of the lion, the calf, man, and the eagle—the recognized heads of the animal creation, " The four forms suggest what is noblest, strongest, wisest and swiftest in animate nature." Their appearance seems to denote that they are the symbols, in some mysterious and profound way, of creation in its manifoldness and greatness. They closely resemble the Cherubim of Ezek. i; but there are marked differences. Those of Ezekiel are seen in the midst of an " infolding fire," which has no parallel in Rev. iv. Ezekiel's has each four wings; these of Rev. have six each. In this they approach the Seraphim of Isa. vi: 2. Both here and in Ezekiel they are associated with the throne of God. In chap. vi: 1-8, they are represented as in some sense the executors of the Divine Will; they summon the four riders with their authoritative *Come*. They appear to be connected with the providential judgments of God, are seen doing the behests of Him who is enthroned, about whom they stand as guards, or like a military staff. They are full of eyes, symbol of wondrous intelligence and sleepless vigilance.

What do they symbolize? Certainly not the Four Gosples, as some suppose; nor four great Apostles; as Peter, James, John, Paul; nor redeemed humanity. They may be symbols either of the Forces of Nature through which God's will is accomplished, or *hieroglyphs* of certain chief attributes; as, righteousness, truth, power and mercy.

The Sealed Book and the Lamb, v: 1-14. The book which John saw was no ordinary roll. It rested on the right hand of Him who sat on the Throne, as if held forth to be taken and opened. It was written both within and on the back; it was close sealed with seven seals. The solemn challenge by a strong angel rang out in heaven, "Who is worthy to open the book, and to loose the seals thereof?" No created being in the whole universe was able to look upon it, much less to open it. One alone was—One with the significant titles, "Lion of the tribe of Judah," "the Root of David," "the Lamb that was slain." It is the Lord Jesus Christ. He is able to take the book, and to loose its seals. For His is the perfection of power; His seven horns denote it; His is the perfection of intelligence; His seven eyes are the proof; His perfect right to sovereignty and supremacy rests in this—He died and rose again; He is the Lamb that was slain. He " hath overcome (Gk. achieved the victory) to open the book and the seven seals thereof."

The meaning of this sublime vision is not far to seek. This chapter, as also the succeeding visions, indicates with unmistakable clearness the significance of the heavenly transaction. There is no hint that the book was read, that its contents were disclosed. We are told of the events which succeed the opening of the seals, but of the contents written within it nothing is said. Did the book contain the events? Doubtful. It would be unwarranted to affirm so much. The august transaction should be studied as a whole, not any particular feature of it.

Beyond all doubt the vision is of transcendent import. Men differ as to what it means and all it means.

The view that commends itself to the writer as being the most satisfactory is this: The Heavenly scene here described represents Christ's investiture of sovereign authority and rule as the rightful Governor of the world, the King and Lord of every realm and of every region. Supreme authority was conferred on Him at His exaltation (Matt. xxviii: 18; Eph. i: 20-23; Phil. ii: 9-11), but He did not at that time take full possession of all His rights and prerogatives; some He held in abeyance. He is now seated at the right hand of the throne of God (Heb. i: 3; xii: 2; Rev. iii. 21 etc.). He is there as Mediator, conducting the vast and manifold interests of His redemptive work. But He is there also " expecting till his enemies be made the footstool of his feet," Heb. x: 12, 13. The 2d and the 110th Psalms expressly teach that a day shall come when God will give to His Son the heathen for His inheritance, and the uttermost parts of the earth for His possession; when He will subdue them all under His feet; when He shall rule in the midst of His enemies, and judge among the nations. Peter affirms that the heavens must receive Christ until the times of restoration of all things (Acts iii: 20, 21). Scripture teaches that there comes a time in the prosecution of His work when Christ will take unto Himself His great power and will reign; when He will put down all authority and rule; when He will establish His glorious Kingdom in victorious power over the entire planet, and He alone will be the King of kings, and the Lord of lords. In this august scene that time has arrived. Christ takes the sealed

book out of the right hand of the Father. It is the
" title-deed " to the inheritance which He has purchased by His obedience unto death, as the Elders and
the Living Beings sing, v: 9: " Worthy art thou to
take the book and to open the seals thereof: for thou
wast slain, and didst purchase unto God with thy
blood," etc. The angelic hosts chant the like song:
" Worthy is the Lamb that hath been slain to receive
the power, and riches, and wisdom, and might, and
honor, and glory, and blessing " (v: 12). Groaning
creation now at length feels the first thrill of the promised deliverance, and sings its glad song of hope and
expectation: " Unto Him that sitteth on the throne,
and unto the Lamb, be the blessing, and the honor, and
the glory, and the dominion, for ever and ever " (v:
13, 14). All created beings join in this glad song,
for the redemption of the purchased possession has
now at length come.

All these tuneful ascriptions of praise to the Lamb
of God attest the profound significance of the heavenly
transaction. A mighty change is here indicated in the
mediatorial work of our Lord. Christ now at length
in infinite majesty and power begins to recover the
alienated inheritance, to clear it of every incumbrance,
to put down every foe, to destroy all hostile forces, and
to rule unchallenged over all. Hitherto He hath been
seated at God's right hand, "expecting," Heb. x: 12.
But in this vision He is seen standing before the
Throne as if the appointed time has come, and the
glorious Kingdom is now to be established, and the
millennium be brought in. Accordingly, it is from

this point that the supreme prophetic action of the book begins its course, and it runs on to the final consummation. Chaps. iv, v, are thus introductory to and explanatory of all that follows, they are essential to any adequate understanding of the book.

Dan. vii: 9-14 points to the same great transaction recorded in Rev. v. One who is named "Ancient of Days" (God the Father) sits upon a Throne from which stream fiery flames, and about which stand thousands upon thousands of angelic hosts ministering unto Him. A secret judgment is pronounced on the Little Horn and the Beast, and the doom of both is irrevocably pronounced, vii: 9-12. Verses 13, 14, introduce a scene marvellously akin to that described in Rev. v: " I saw in the night visions, and, behold, there came with the clouds of heaven one like unto a son of man, and he came even to the ancient of Days, and they brought him near before him. And there was given him dominion, and glory, and a kingdom, that all peoples, nations and languages should serve him," cf. vers. 26, 27. The Son of Man, Jesus Christ, is here represented as coming into the place of judicature, and there receiving investiture of the everlasting Kingdom. His investiture immediately precedes His coming forth to crush the Beast, to annihilate the Antichrist (the Little Horn), and His taking the Kingdom for the saints of the Most High. This vision in Daniel appears to be exactly parallel with that of John.

The parable of the Nobleman (Luke xix: 11-27) points to the same supreme event as the vision of Daniel. "A certain nobleman went into a far country to receive for himself a kingdom, and to return . . . And it came to pass, when he was come back again, having received the kingdom," etc. No one can question that the Nobleman represents Christ Himself. The far country to which He went is heaven. The kingdom He went to receive is the same glorious kingdom predicted in Dan. vii, " a kingdom that all people, nations, and languages should serve him." The parable teaches that this kingdom shall come to victorious power over all the earth, when the King Himself, the Lord Jesus Christ, shall " return." The words, " having received the kingdom," seem to denote His investiture of the kingdom, His right and title to take it, and to establish His sovereign rule over the world.

We conclude, therefore, that this majestic scene so graphically portrayed in Rev. v, when the Lamb that was slain, the Lion of the Tribe of Judah, receives investiture of the kingdom, has not yet taken place. The proof of this statement is twofold: (a) the successive opening of the seven Seals is connected with the Coming of the Lord at the time of the End. The sixth and the seventh Seals make this absolutely certain. No time seems to elapse between taking the book and opening the Seals. Upon taking the book He at once proceeds to open its Seals. But the opening of the Seals ushers in the " signs " which immediately precede the Advent, Rev. vi: 12-17; viii: 5; Matt. xxiv: 29-31; Mar. xiii: 24-27; Lu. xxi: 25-28.

(b) Both Daniel (vii) and the Lord (Lu. xix) connect the triumphant establishment of the Kingdom over all the world with Christ's Coming. Hence, the investiture immediately precedes the Advent.

CHAPTER VIII.

Mighty movements on earth follow the successive breaking of the Seals. At the repeated cry of the Living Creatures, Come, four horsemen in rapid succession set forth on their mission. Each is distinguished from the others by the color of his horse and by what he carries. The first rider has a bow, his horse is white, and to him as an unfailing conqueror a crown is given. He is a victorious, military chieftain. The second carries a great sword, his horse is red, and it is given him to take peace from the earth. He is the personification of war. The third rides a black horse, and bears a pair of ballances. He prefigures famine, scarcity, though it is not altogether total. The fourth rider is Death, and Hades as a devouring demon follows at his heels; his horse is pale, and he has power to kill with the sword, and with hunger, and with death (or pestilence), and with the wild beasts.

What do these strange, mystic horsemen signify? What do they represent? Of course they are symbolic, and must be so understood, but they are intended to picture a dread reality; they are to have their realization in historical time. To interpret it as a vision of the victorious Christ by His Gospel subduing the world is totally inappropriate, for the whole

68

series of horsemen, as well as the other Seals, are connected with war, bloodshed, famine, pestilence, and death. This cannot be the image of the gracious Prince of Peace sending forth by His messengers the Gospel of His grace. Rather we have here a picture of triumphant militarism. Matt. xxiv: 5-14 brings no little aid to the understanding of this vision. Our Lord tells us that there shall come false Christs (the first rider amazingly resembles a mock Messiah), and there shall be wars, and famines, and pestilence, and earthquakes, nations shall be in commotion and revolution, and God's people shall suffer tribulation and martyrdom—an event connecting at once with the opening of the fifth Seal (ver. 9). " But the end is not yet;" " these are the beginning of sorrows."

These verses of the Olivet Prophecy seem to belong to the time of Jerusalem's overthrow, A. D. 79, as Luke reporting the same Discourse of the Lord plainly says, Lu. xxi: 8-20. There can be no doubt that the Lord Jesus had in mind the troublous times that preceded and accompanied the capture of Jerusalem by the Romans under Titus, the horrible sufferings then endured by uncounted multitudes of Jews, and afflictions and slaughter of His own disciples, as the book of the Acts, and the later Epistles of Paul, and those of Peter, and Jude abundantly attest. But do those events, can they exhaust His predictions? Did wars, famines, pestilences, false prophets and false Messiahs end with the destruction of the holy city of Israel? No one would be so foolish as to assert it. The like things, in a little less than seventy

years after, reappeared in the rebellion of the im-
poster, Bar-Cochba, who, with his following, was
overthrown by the Emperor Hadrian, Jerusalem was
laid in heaps, and its ruins sown with salt. In almost
every century since the like commotions, and dis-
turbances, and bloodshed have been repeated. It must
be borne in mind that two prime objects were
before our Lord's mind when He predicted the events
of Matt. xxiv, viz.: Jerusalem's ruin and His Second Coming. The one object glides into the other,
both events have some things which precede them in
common. His prophecy is a *double one*, applying
both to Jerusalem and His Advent. Accordingly, we
believe that before He comes to earth again, and,
perhaps, not long before, the like things that presaged
Jerusalem's destruction will announce in the most
solemn fashion the nearness of His appearing. History repeates itself. Our age, the Gospel age, began
at Jerusalem; prophetic Scripture appears to testify
that it will terminate there.

If the right interpretation has been given to the
Lamb's taking the Book from the hand of Him who
sat on the throne and opening its Seals, then the
action of the four riders does not relate to Jerusalem's
desolation, nor to the suffering then endured. The
action of the horsemen belongs to the time of the
End, to the last mighty conflict between the Son of
Man and the hostile powers of the world. When these
riders start forth portentous movements are afield;
the forces are marching and massing for the final
struggle. We think they go forth before Daniel's

Seventieth Week begins its course. They clear the way for the monster Beast and his ten confederate kings. A heavenly mandate seems to summon them, and providence permits them to work their will, for restraints will then be withdrawn and the forces of the End-time will do as they list. The Living Beings that call them out are intimately associated with the Throne of God and its decrees, Rom. ix: 28.

The fifth Seal is the martyr Seal, vi: 9-11. The Seer saw " under the altar the souls of them that were slain for the word of God, and for the testimony which they held." Their blood had been poured out like that of sacrificial victims at the altar's bottom. They were slain for the same cause that banished John to the desolate Patmos, i: 9; " for the word of God, and for the testimony of Jesus Christ." They were Christian martyrs no less than was John a Christian sufferer. It is held that these martyrs do not pertain to the Church, for their cry, " How long, O, Lord, holy and true, dost thou not judge and avenge our blood on them that dwell on the earth ?" —indicates they are on other ground than Christian. This view is maintained mainly to save the theory that the Rapture of the Church occurs at the opening of the fourth chapter of our book, and as this scene is subsequent thereto, these martyrs are not of the Body. But almost precisely the same language is employed by our Lord in Luke xviii: 7, "And shall not God avenge his own elect who cry day and night unto him, though he bear long with them ? " It would be presumptuous to deny the application of these words to Christians. The context settles that matter. The method of interpretation which deftly puts an inconvenient text out of the way so as to save the view is perilously close to that of the rationalist who says of Scripture that cuts across his theory, "It is spurious," "an interpolation," "it don't apply." Why try to rob these martyrs of their heritage? If they are not members of the Body, neither is John, for he and they stand precisely on the same ground, suffer for the same reason—"the word of God and the testimony of Jesus Christ." All the Seals pertain to the time just before Christ's Advent.

The martyrdom of these saints post-dates the summons to the four horsemen. For aught told us to the contrary, they were slain by the order of these riders. Persecution, no doubt, deepens and intensifies through the sanguinary and cruel action of the horsemen. Hence, other martyrs are to follow them. These must wait till their brethren have been put to death before God will execute judgment on their murderers. This fact, as already intimated, obviously links these sufferers with all who succeed them, including no doubt those of the Great Tribulation itself.

These and all other martyrs of Christ will have a triumphant vindication in due time, cf. xi: 18. They will be raised up, and will live and reign with Christ a thousand years, xx: 4, 5. "This is the first resurrection." So the Spirit of God witnesses. No resurrection of saint or martyr takes place before this, else it could not by any possibility be called "the first resurrection." It occurs when Christ returns to earth in visible majesty and overwhelming power and glory, as chap. xix: 11-21 so graphically reveals. As we read it, the Apocalypse has no other resurrection, knows no other resurrection than this " first."

The opening of the sixth Seal is succeeded by extraordinary convulsions of nature and universal consternation of men, vi: 12-17. These are the " signs " which immediately precede the Advent of Christ. It is " the Day of the Lord," the Day of most appalling phenomena, as the prophets testify, cf. Isa. xiii: 9, 10; Joel ii; 30, 31; iii: 14-16; Zeph. i: 14-18; Zech. xiv: 6, 7, etc. The signs are the precursor of the visible appearing of Jesus Christ. They precede the actual Coming by the briefest space of time, and they immediately follow the Great Tribulation. Our Lord foretells this " sign-time " in graphic terms, Matt. xxiv: 29; Luke xxi: 25-28. Nothing in the world's history has yet happened which on any fair principle of interpretation even approaches the fulfilment of the contents of this sixth Seal. The conversion of Constantine, the fall of the Roman Empire, the irruption of the Barbarians, the French Revolution—not one of these events, nor all of them combined, are anywhere near an accomplishment of the " signs," else, as one tersely puts it, " the majesty of the prediction is lost in the poverty of its fulfilment."

The opening of the seventh Seal is the consummation, viii: 1, 5.

THE EPISODE OF THE SEALED AND THE SAVED, chap. **vii.**

As already noted, this episode is introduced between the sixth and the seventh Seals. But the time covered by it is certainly more than the brief space which lies between the " sign-time " and the Advent. It appears to us that it stretches over the period between the first and the last of the Seals. The world movements and the activities of the great adversary are shown us in the first five Seals; the episode discloses to us God's activities and mercies in grace in this same period. First, 144,000 of Israel's tribes are sealed with the seal of God (cf. Ezek. ix). They are Jews, the seed of Abraham, for they stand in sharp contrast with the saved from among the Gentiles, vs. 9-17. Two companies, quite distinct from one another, are here brought to view, viz.: the 144,000 (square of 12,000) sealed out of Israel, and the innumerable hosts gathered from among the nations, v: 9. The purpose of the sealing is to secure these chosen Hebrews against the wrath which is about to be poured out on the ungodly. Hence, the four angels standing on earth's " four corners " are bidden to hold back the judgments until these are safe under the seal of God. The same company appears under the sounding of the fifth Trumpet, and they are preserved from its desolation because they have as here in the episode the seal of God in their foreheads (ix: 4). It is difficult to locate the time of the sealing, but it seems almost certain it belongs to a point before the Tribulation begins, for these believing Jews are no doubt the fruit of the testimony of the Two Witnesses (xi), and if so, their sealing belongs to the time of the four riders (vi:1-8).

Second, an innumerable host of saved Gentiles are seen in glory, before the throne of God, clad in white raiment, with palm branches in their hands. They have come to their place of bliss through the "great tribulation" (the Greek is most emphatic, "the tribulation the great one"). It is one of unprecedented trouble, of unparalleled suffering. Daniel speaks of it as a "time of trouble, such as never was since there was a nation even to that same time" (Dan. xii: 1). Jeremiah also, "Alas! for that day is great, so that none is like it; it is even the time of Jacob's trouble; but he shall be saved out of it" (Jer. xxx: 7). Christ likewise, "For then shall be great tribulation, such as hath not been from the beginning of the world until now; no, nor ever shall be" (Matt. xxiv: 21). Never yet has this tribulation, so unequalled in intensity and awfulness taken place. It is still future, but as seen in this vision the saved have passed through it, and are now in glory. The sealed 144,000 seem to have been preserved through it, sheltered from its dreadfulness by the seal of God.

It is the judgment of trustworthy interpreters of prophecy that the last or Seventieth Week of Daniel's mystic Seventy has never yet run its course in human history, Dan. ix: 24-27. It still belongs to the future. The Week consists of seven years of literal time. The prophets divide it into two equal parts of three and one-half years each, Dan. vii: 25; xii: 7; Rev. xii: 14.

Each half of the Week is also spoken of as forty-two months, Rev. xi: 2; xiii: 5, and as 1,260 days, Rev. xi: 3; xii: 6. The following diagram may serve to illustrate the divided Week:

DANIEL'S SEVENTIETH WEEK—SEVEN YEARS.

3½ years years, Dan. xii: 7.	3½ years, Rev. xii: 14.
42 months, Rev. xi: 2.	42 months, Rev. xiii: 5.
1,260 days, Rev. xi: 3.	1,260 days, Rev. xii: 6.

The numbers of each half of the Week, though expressed in years, months, and days, designate the same period—three and a half years twice over, seven years in all. We believe this to be literal time.

The world's crisis, the culmination of evil, the tremendous judgments of God, the First Resurrection and the inauguration of the Millennium are all narrowed into the compass of these seven years of time. Israel's age-long exile and suffering will then terminate in their restoration to God, and their reinstatement in the divine favor, nevermore to be rejected and cast off. But these seven years will mark momentous events, unexampled suffering, colossal wickedness, and the wrath of God poured out to the uttermost.

It is difficult, if not impossible, accurately to say just what events will take place in each part of this divided Week, these seven years. It must be kept in mind that the outburst of godlessness, which will then reach its climax, has had a gradual development, has long been gathering force and ripening. As an ancient writer expresses it, "The road is long in preparing, but the end of it is sudden and swift." It is quite possible that the first four Seals lie before the Seven Years begin their course. The fifth Seal belongs in part to each half, for there will no doubt be martyrs, both in the one and in the other. There is little doubt but that the Two Witnesses (Rev. xi) testify during the first half of the Week, and die before the events of the second half begin their course. The Tribulation is certainly in the second half. The Beast appears in the first half when he slays the Witnesses; he comes to the summit of his bad pre-eminence in the second. Israel is in both halves, as also are Gentile believers. There will be a martyred remnant of Israel, and also a spared remnant. It is the spared remnant that is sealed and kept during the time of trouble. The unnumbered throng of Gentile martyrs are in this episode seen in glory: resurrection accordingly for them is here prospectively accomplished. There will also be a sheltered remnant of Gentile saints, Rev. iii: 10.

CHAPTER IX.

THE SEVEN TRUMPETS, viii: 6—xi: 18.

Like the Vials, the Trumpets are judicial; they inflict judgment on the wicked and the ungodly of the time of the end. The first four smite, not guilty man directly, but certain objects of nature which are essential to man's well-being. The first strikes vegetation; the second the sea; the third the rivers and fountains of waters; the fourth the sun, moon, and stars. These beneficent powers of nature, on which man is so dependent for his well-being, are stripped of one-third of their energy under the judgments of God. Through nature God chastises the ungodly. If they should bow to His rod and repent, no doubt the judgments would be removed. But the two Woe Trumpets which deal directly with men, and inflict on them the heaviest punishments, prove they do not repent, they grew worse and worse (ix: 20, 21). The Trumpets do not begin to sound at the same point where the Seals begin. The first Trumpet apparently starts where the third Seal ends and the fourth begins. They all, however, terminate at the same point—the consummation.

The fifth Trumpet (ix: 1-11; 1st Woe) brings a fearful scourge upon the earth. It seems to involve all men and nature in its sweep. There are two exemptions, however, the "locusts" from the smoke of the pit must not hurt vegetation, nor touch the men who had the seal of God in their forehead, ver. 4. On the others the blow falls with utmost violence, and with crushing effect, so that the guilty sufferers seek death and do not find it, death flies from them. The torture lasts for five months.

The historical interpreters find the fulfilment of this vision of the scorpion-like locusts in the Saracen armies, the Fallen Star being their prophet, Mohammed. Others regard these scourges as the armies of heretics and infidels; others still, as swarms of demons let loose on the guilty world, their king and leader being no other than the devil himself. Not one of these interpretations is satisfactory. That of the historical school has historical ground for it. There is a remarkable parallelism between the prediction here and the rise and progress of Islam. Even William Kelly, a staunch futurist, does not shrink from saying, " I do not doubt that the common *application* of the locusts to the Saracens, and of the Euphratean horsemen to the Turks is well founded." The difficulty lies in this, the Woe Trumpets sound at the time of the end, in Daniel's Seventieth Week, and hence events which occurred a thousand years ago cannot possibly exhaust this mighty prophecy. They adumbrate it, but are not its complete fulfilment.

The following explanation of this vision is defferentially submitted. The key to its meaning is found in the phrase of ver. 4, " men who have not the seal of God in their foreheads." Those who have that seal are exempt from the judgment which now

falls. The reference must be to the 144,000 sealed of
vii: 1-8. They are Hebrews, and the seal shields
them from the " torment " of the invading army here
foretold. At the time of the vision Israel in large
numbers is back in the Land; most of them are unbelieving, some of them have become the true people
of God. These are protected, those are exposed to
the fury of the invading host. That host, it is believed, is identical with Ezekiel's Gog, prince of Rosh,
Meshech, and Tubal, Ezek. xxxviii: lxxxix; Joel ii.
Ezekiel's prophecy locates the time " in that day,"
xxxviii: 10, 14, " when my people Israel dwelleth
securely." In Joel it is the Day of the Lord, ii: 1. In
Joel the army resembles locusts in the suddenness of
their appearance, their countless numbers, their irre-
sistible progress, and their insatiable rapacity. But
they do not prey on the sealed of God, they do not
touch earth's vegetation, they smite the unbelieving
among men. It is quite possible Russia will have the
chief part in this invasion, but she will not be alone
in it. Swarms of other peoples will also engage in it,
as Ezekiel clearly announces. All these invaders,
this huge host of Gog, will be animated by a satanic
spirit, and will be filled with the fury of demons.
They bring with them the smoke of the Pit. The
plague is of but short duration, it lasts but five
months, ix: 5.

The sixth Trumpet, vision of the Euphratean Horse-
men, ix: 13-21. This is the second of the Woe
Trumpets, and, like the first, it must be one of calamity.
Such it assuredly is. By this countless army of 200,-

000,000, ver. 16, the third part of men are killed. No exemption of the sealed of God is made, nor of earth's productions, as in the case of the other Woe; the terrific judgment here falls with merciless force. The language of course is symbolical. The four angels, "bound" perhaps, mean the providential restraints of armed forces from the East. The Euphrates connects the thought with Babylon, and Babylon is directly associated with the Beast, chap. xvii. It may, therefore, be that it is the imperial army of the Antichrist, provoked by the coming into Palestime of the king of the North with his hordes, as the prophets reveal (Ezek. xxxviii: 6, 15; Dan. xi: 40; Joel ii: 20). Daniel, in chap. xi: 40-45, predicts the invasion of Palestine by the wilful king (the Beast or Antichrist), and the attack on him by the kings of the north and the south, and apparently the king's victory over those combined forces. It may be that this vast army (we think the number 200,000,000 is ideal, not literal, denoting an extraordinary large army) will consist mainly of Mohammedans, who in that day will combine against the Wilful King, who will then be seeking the subjugation of the whole earth. Surely that dreadful scourge of the ages, Mohammedanism, will hold a conspicuous place in the scenes of the last days. Its dark record of despotism, desolation, ravage and slaughter, will, possibly, end with one supreme effort to regain its vanishing power and its lost territories. But certainty as to the full significance of this vision of the Euphratean army is at present unattainable. The historical in-

6

terpreters find its fulfilment in the invasion of western Asia by the Turks, which resulted in the capture of Constantinople (A. D. 1453). There is a remarkable parallelism between the prediction as thus viewed and the historical facts. It can hardly be doubted but that it then received a partial and anticipatory accomplishment. But the vision belongs specifically to the time of the end. It may be that *then* Islam will put forth its last and most vigorous exertion to preserve its existence, and thus fulfil this vision.

The locust-like army of the fifth Trumpet torment men with their sting. The Euphratean horsemen kill the third part of men. The scourge lasts for a definite period; namely, " the hour, and day, and month, and year." Its beginning, duration, and end are fixed by divine decree. That this great army is *human,* and not a countless multitude of evil spirits as some think, seems to us certain. It must be constantly borne in mind that the movements of nations and of men in the last times will be on a scale of vastness almost beyond what we can now conceive. Prophecy appears to involve the whole world in the revolutions and convulsions of those days.

The third Woe Trumpet, xi: 15-19—the seventh and last. Heavenly voices announce, " The kingdom of the world has become *the kingdom* of our Lord and of His Christ; and He shall reign for ever and ever," xi: 15, R. V. The world-kingdom has now become the Lord's, so the words signify. Obviously, this is the final consummation, the End. Accordingly, the twenty-four Elders say, " Thou hast taken thy great power and didst reign. And the nations were wroth, and thy wrath came, and the time of the dead to be judged, and the time to give their reward to thy servants the prophets, and to the saints, and to them that fear thy name, the small and the great; and to destroy them that destroy the earth," vers. 16-18. This language unmistakably denotes the time of the End. It is very notable. (1) The rage of the nations, (2) God's wrath visited upon them, (3) resurrection and vindication of the saints, (4) distribution of rewards among God's people, (5) overthrow of earth's destroyers. We do not think that the wicked share in this resurrection. The term "Judged" means to judge with the purpose of vindication, and the dead thus judged are described as exclusively belonging to God. There is no hint here of the presence of the wicked dead. The righteous alone are here, to whom the blessed Judge gives His gracious rewards. The seventh Trumpet is the last and the resurrection trumpet, 1 Cor. xv: 52.

The words of the Elders are noteworthy, "We give thee thanks, O Lord God, the Almighty, who art and who wast," xi: 17. The clause "and art to come" is omitted in the Revisions, and in all the late critical Greek texts (Alford, Wescott & Hort, Weymouth, and Nestle). In i: 4, 8, ; iv: 8, the ascription is, "Who was, and who is, and who is to come," or "who cometh." But here in xi: 17 the final clause is omitted, "who cometh." Why? Manifestly because the Lord actually comes when the seventh

Trumpet sounds. In iv: 8 He has **not** come, **He is**
still the coming One.

THE EPISODE, chaps. x-xi: 14.

This episode, like that of the Seals, is interposed
between the sixth and the seventh Trumpet. Space
will allow but brief remarks on three subjects in these
chapters. (1.) The Oath of the Angel and his solemn
proclamation, x: 5-7. His imposing attitude, his up-
lifted right hand, and his appeal to Him who is the
Living One, attest the momentousness and truth of
his announcement, " There shall be no longer delay."
Not that time is then to end and eternity begin, but
that God will now at length interpose and put an end
to the lawlessness and the crimes of the world. The
angel asserts that this interposition will take place at
the sounding of the seventh Trumpet; then the mystery of God will be finished—the secret of His letting His foes have their own way and of letting the
bad triumph and the good be trodden underfoot.
All this will terminate with the 7th Trumpet, xi: 1-18.

(2.) The temple and the holy city, xi: 1, 2. These
certainly cannot be the heavenly temple and city, nor
the Christian church. For " the court " is cast out
as unholy and polluted. No chronological scheme can
be devised for the past or the present that will give
42 months of desolation either for the church or the
earthly Jerusalem. The two Witnesses have never
yet appeared in connection with Jerusalem and the
Jews; but the temple, the city and the testimony **of**

the witnesses are certainly connected with the land of Palestine, and particularly with Jerusalem. Nor has the Beast appeared, nor have the witnesses been slain by him. Accordingly, it seems to us that beyond peradventure what is foretold in this episode belongs to the future, and the scenes and events announced in it will take place in the days of the Seals, the Trumpets and Vials, i. e., at the End.

(3.) The Two Witnesses, xi: 3-13. God will never leave Himself without a witness even in the dreadful times of the End. Before the final deliverance arrives for Israel two Witnesses will testify for God in the midst of Jerusalem, and miraculous powers will once more be exhibited among the chosen people. We are not told who these Witnesses are nor whence. The account given of them is brief but rich in suggestion. They are clothed in sackcloth, emblem of humiliation and of affliction; their ministry is one of appeal and denunciation, hence calculated to arouse antagonism. "These are the two olive trees and the two candlesticks, standing before the Lord of the earth" (cf. Zech. iv: 3, 11, 14). They are anointed for an extraordinary work, and they are endued with supernatural power to execute it. They can shut heaven, and they can smite men. Their ministry lasts for 1260 days, i. e., three and a half years, when they are slain by the Beast, and their bodies are refused burial. How bitter must be the hostility against them! After three and a half days they are raised up, and summoned to heaven by a "great voice," "Come up hither!"

Are these witnesses two individual men? So the passage appears to teach. Many, however, think they represent two companies of witnesses, at the head of which two men stand as chief. Even some staunch futurists, as James Smith and William Kelly, incline to this view. The majority believe that they are in reality but two individual men. Some suppose they are Enoch and Elijah; others, Moses and Elijah. The only evidence in support of the opinion is the miracles wrought by them are closely akin to those of Moses and Elijah. Beyond this there is not a hint that they are sent to earth from the unseen world. It is extremely improbable that these saints, after centuries of bliss in heaven, should be dispatched to earth to bear witness to Jews and Gentiles. The passage does not require such an interpretation. All it demands is, that the witnesses be invested with supernatural authority and with miraculous power. John the Baptist is an analogous instance of such witness-bearing. He came in the " spirit and power of Elijah " (Lu. i: 17). Jesus said of him—" That Elijah is indeed come, and they have done unto him whatsoever they listed " (Matt. xvii: 12). But John was not Elijah. He might have done all predicted of Elijah had the Jews received him and his testimony (Matt. xi: 14). If two men shall appear in the last days, as these two assuredly will, and bear the witness of God to rebellious men in the spirit and power of Moses and Elijah, the terms of this prophecy will be met.

The historical interpretators cite a striking instance

of the accomplishment of xi: 3-13, according to their method of exposition. In A. D. 1512-17 the Fifth Lateran Council was held in Rome. A papal bull was issued in December, 1513, which commanded all dissidents from papal authority to appear in due time before the Council, and show cause for their refusal to acknowledge the pope's supremacy. When the time appointed arrived to hear such cause, no answer to Leo's summons appeared. The orator of that session (May, 1514) uttered, amidst the applause of the Council, the memorable exclamation, " There is an end of resistance to the papal rule and religion; opposers exist no more!" Evangelical testimony was hushed! Three years and a half later, almost to a day (October, 1517) Luther nailed his theses to the Wittenberg church-door! It looks much as if the witnesses were indeed slain, but they gloriously revive in the power of the great Reformation. We have no good reason to reject this application of the prophecy as a partial and proleptic fulfilment. But it does not meet all the facts. The witnesses beyond question prosecute their ministry in Jerusalem, and there they are slain, xi: 8. Besides, the Beast, it seems to us, cannot be merely a corrupt and apostate ecclesiastical system like Popery; he comes from the " abyss;" he is, or seems to be, a man, not only an organization such as Romanism is. Furthermore, the witnesses appear just before the seventh Trumpet sounds when the consummation is reached and the Son of Man, Jesus Christ, comes and establishes His Kingdom over the world.

Apparently the ministry of the two witnesses ends

in total failure. But the failure is only apparent. The most blessed results follow the testimony which brought them to martyrdom. We have no doubt that the conversion of Israel's remnant of sealed ones (vii: 1-8) is the glorious issue of their work as the following chapters appear to indicate.

CHAPTER X.

The Intercalated Visions, chaps. xii, xiii, xiv.

With this great section the student is confronted by some of the most intricate and perplexing problems of the Apocalypse. Help from books of a substantial sort is painfully meagre. The more one reads the less certainty he has as to its meaning. Happy he who catches glimpses of the massive truth hidden behind the stupendous imagery of this section of Revelation! Let it be ours to cautiously thread our way through the intricacies of these chapters, seeking to grasp only the prominent things signified in them and passing by details of exposition.

Chap. xii has two " signs "—a sun-clothed Woman and a great, red dragon. Our first inquiry relates to this " sign " of the Woman. Who is she? What does she represent? The conjectures of writers are multitudinous and generally contradictory. We need not burden the page with enumerating them. We assume that she is not the Virgin Mary, for the history of our Saviour's mother does not correspond with what is told us of this sun-clothed woman. She is not the Christian Church, for in no proper or adequate sense can we affirm that she gives birth to the Man-Child who was to rule all nations with a rod of iron, and who was caught up to the throne of God. It is by Messiah the Church is born, certainly not by the Church Messiah becomes incarnate. The Church in all ages and generations is composed of members who are brought into it by the Spirit of God, and one by one, individually. The Woman here gives birth to one majestic and glorious Son; the event is consummated at once, not prolonged through ages, as is the case with the Christian Church, and even with the Jewish Church.

We believe that the key to the significance of this great " sign " is found in the 19th verse of the preceding chapter. After the seventh Trumpet has sounded and the consummation is at length come, the Seer goes back and starts once more with a fresh vision, which leads him into the marvellous revelations contained in these chapters. In xi: 19 we read: "And the temple (sanctuary) of God was opened in heaven, and there was seen in his temple the ark of the covenant." This is strictly Jewish ground; the temple, the ark, the covenant belong to Israel, represent Hebrew relations with God and Hebrew privileges. The Spirit now takes up Jewish things, Jewish standing, covenant, hopes, dangers, tribulations and triumph. The verse connects with what follows, is introductory to it—is explanatory also. The Man-Child is certainly the Lord Jesus Christ. The woman is not a literal female; she is the symbol of the Messianic nation, the Daughter of Zion; for through her, Israel, Christ was given to the world (Rom. ix: 5). But the prophet is not here tracing Israel's history, nor that of Israel's Messiah; this is not his theme. In a magnificent picture he sets forth Israel's connection with

Messiah, first, in His incarnation, and second, the conversion of the first instalment, the firstfruits of the chosen people to God, vii: 1-8; xiv: 1-5. The chapter touches the first Advent, then sketches the events that pertain to the time of the second Advent.

The Dragon is the old Serpent, the Devil and Satan, xii: 9. Full of hatred against the Woman, Israel, whom he has never ceased to persecute, whose Son he sought to slay at Bethlehem, he now appears in his last disguise. He is seen as a huge Dragon, half serpent and half wild beast, with seven crowned heads and ten horns. His outward form links him at once with the revived World Empire, as chap. xiii unmistakably proves. Neither Rome pagan or papal ever had such disguise; never yet has appeared a power with seven heads and ten horns, or with what this symbol portrays. Beyond question the apparition of this monster, energized as he will be by the Devil, belongs to the future. An event of worldwide import precedes or accompanies the appearing of the seven-headed monster on earth. "And there was war in heaven: Michael and his angels fought against the dragon; and the dragon fought, and his angels, and prevailed not; neither was their place found any more in heaven. And the great dragon was cast out," xii: 7-9, Cf. Dan. xii: 1, 2. Immediately upon the dejection of the great adversary from "heaven" to earth a shout of gladness rings through heaven, "Now is come salvation, and strength, and the kingdom of our God, and the power of his Christ: for the accuser of our brethren is cast down, which accuseth them be-

fore our God day and night," ver. 10. The ground of
Satan's accusation is human unfaithfulness, unbelief;
in Israel's case, apostasy. So long as the Jews remain obdurate and apostate from God and from His
Messiah, so long the enemy holds his vantage ground.
But what is it which brings about his dejection? In
Dan. xii: 1 it is Michael who "stands up, the great
prince which standeth for the children of thy people"
(Daniel's people). In Rev. xii: 7, 8 it is likewise
Michael fighting against the dragon and overcoming
him. But more is told us: "And they overcame him
by the blood of the Lamb, and by the word of their
testimony; and they loved not their lives unto the
death." These are saints on earth who have come to
faith in Jesus Christ, who receive Him as Saviour,
and who bear faithful witness to Him in the midst of
trial and affliction. They are Jewish believers, and
their conversion seems to synchronize with the "war
in heaven."

The words of other prophets confirm and explain
these symbolic pictures. Micah predicts the first advent of the Redeemer, then foretells Israel's rejection
and restoration: "Therefore will he give them up,
until the time that she which travaileth hath brought
forth: then the residue of his brethren shall return
unto the children of Israel" (v: 2, 3). Isaiah speaks
of the same event: "Before she travailed she brought
forth; before her pain came she was delivered of a
man-child. Shall a nation be born in one day? For
as soon as Zion travailed she brought forth her children" (lxvi: 7, 8). Israel's conversion, even as to

the "firstfruits," the 144,000 of sealed ones, as we think is here specially meant, precipitates the crisis. Satan, cast down from his high place of accusation, rages on earth, persecutes the Woman and goes to make war with the remnant of her seed, who keep the commandments of God, and hold the testimony of Jesus, xii: 17.

According to Daniel, when Michael " stands up " for Israel, the time of unprecedented trouble begins (xii: 1, 2). According to John, when saints overcome the Dragon because of the blood of the Lamb and of the word of their testimony, the seven-headed and ten-horned Foe furiously assails the Woman and the remnant of her seed who believe. It is the opening of the Great Tribulation, the time of Jacob's " trouble." But if the Dragon is busy God is even busier. If the one determines the annihilation of the Woman, the Other determines to save her. And so she is given two wings of a great eagle whereby she flies into the wilderness, where God has provided for her a place of safety and of nourishment during the whole period of the Tribulation, three and a half years. The flight is from Jerusalem and Judea; it is also from the deadly wrath of the Beast, the Antichrist, Satan's agent and tool. It is, we do not doubt, the sealed company of believing Israelites, the 144,-000 of chap. vii and chap. xiv, who flee for safety. God provides for their safety.

John is not alone in this prediction. Other prophets refer to the same event. Thus Zechariah announces that the nations shall be gathered together against Jerusalem, that the city shall be taken and plundered, that half its population shall go into captivity, but "the residue of the people shall not be cut off from the city." God in a most marvellous manner will interpose in behalf of His suffering remnant, and will cleave out of the mountain of Olives a valley of escape; and the prophet adds: "And ye shall flee by the valley of my mountains; for the valley of the mountains shall reach unto Azel: yea, ye shall flee, like as ye fled from before the earthquake in the days of Uzziah king of Judah; and Jehovah my God shall come, and all the holy ones with thee," Zech. xiv: 1-5. Daniel (xi: 41) declares that "the King," the Antichrist, will be prevented from taking Edom, Moab, and Ammon. All other lands will fall under his victorious arms. These shall escape. May it be that it is to this rocky, almost inaccessible territory the saved remnant will flee? Cf. Psa. lx: 9-11.

Foiled in the effort to destroy the Woman, the furious Dragon turns his rage against the rest of her seed who "keep the commandments of God, and hold the testimony of Jesus," xii: 17. These are believing Jews, and seem to constitute the martyred remnant of the Tribulation. Believing Gentiles will also suffer; perhaps the countless throng of vii: 9-14.

The sum of the teaching of this profound and difficult vision we conceive to be the following:

1. The Sun-clothed Woman is Israel, the Daughter of Zion, seen mainly in the time of the End. She is the Messianic Mother.

2. The Dragon is the Devil, disguised in his last,

his most effective, and yet most hideous mask he has ever worn.

3. "War in heaven" describes Satan's expulsion from his place of eminence and power, and the crisis of the world immediately ensues.

4. Security of the mystic Woman, Israel's sealed company.

5. War against the Woman's seed, Israel's martyred remnant.

6. Martyrdom of the countless throng of Gentile believers, vii: 9-14.

The conversion of Israel's "firstfruits," the sealed company of 144,000, and the dejection of the old Serpent from heaven synchronize. It is this conversion of Israel's sealed and martyred remnants which destroys the devil's ground of accusation against the saints, and forshortens the period of his malignant activity; but it intensifies his rage.

THE TWO WILD BEASTS, Chap. xiii.

"And he stood upon the sand of the sea" (xiii: 1 R. V.). It is the Dragon that thus stands by the seashore. Defeated in his efforts to "drown" the Woman (xii: 15, 16), i. e., Israel's newly converted "firstfruits," Satan now calls into action his two agents and allies, the Beast and the False Prophet. Out of the sea the first wild beast rises (cf. Dan. vii: 2). The sea torn by the winds is the lively image of nations and peoples in commotion and revolution. It is out of a disrupted condition of civil society this huge

Beast comes into being. It is out of such a state imperialism always originates. By these two formidable agents, the reorganized imperial World-sovereignty and the False Prophet, the devil will make war against the Woman's seed, seek to destroy Israel, and so thwart the gracious purposes of the Son of God.

The Beast from the sea is the heir and successor of Daniel's four, which are symbols of successive empires or kingdoms (Dan. vii: 17, 23)—the Babylonian, Medo-Persian, Greco-Macedonian, and Roman. This is evident from the composition of John's great symbol. The lion, the bear, the leopard, and the ten-horned monster, each distinct in Daniel, are all united in one in John's, xiii: 2. He has seven heads and ten horns with ten diadems on his horns. The great red dragon of xii: 3 has the same number of heads and horns. Are there, then, two separate powers, the Dragon and the Beast, in the field of action at the same time? Certainly not. When first seen by John in his vision, the Dragon has the symbolic form of the Beast; he has seven heads and ten horns; but he transfers his " power, and his throne, and great authority " (xiii: 2) to his ungodly agent. It is through this new force the devil will exert all his energy and vent all his rage.

The seven heads represent seven kings or kingdoms (Dan. vii: 17, 23; Rev. xvii: 10). Five of them had fallen when John wrote, the sixth, the Roman Empire, was then dominant over most of earth. A seventh kingdom, universal in its sway and altogether satanic in its origin and character, was to come and was to endure for a short space, Rev. xvii: 10. One of the heads, presumably the sixth, the Roman, was seen wounded unto death. It fell beneath the victorious swords of the so-called Barbarians, the Goths, Vandals, Huns, and other foes, and it ceased to be. But it is to be restored to life; the Seer adds, it " shall come," or, as the Sinai MS. expressively reads, " it shall be present again." A worldwide sovereignty, energized by Satan and his most obedient tool, is yet to arise. We hold that these seven heads or empires of the Beast from the sea are not seven forms of rule of the Roman State, as many writers affirm; e. g., kings, consuls, decemvirs, military tribunes, dictators, emperors. They are successive empires; they stand for those world-powers that have been the oppressors and persecutors of God's people. We believe they symbolize the following kingdoms: Egypt, Assyria, Babylon, Medo-Persia, Greece, Rome. This view is confirmed by the fact that in John's huge Beast all the characteristic features of Daniel's four Brutes are found (cf. Dan. vii: 1-7; Rev. xiii: 2). These six Powers have long since disappeared. No world-sovereignty has there been since the fall of the Roman Empire. Ambitious soldiers like Charlemagne and the first Napoleon have attempted the formation of one universal government with himself at its head; but they have utterly failed. Prophecy distinctly announces that one vast united kingdom shall yet arise. It will come at the time of the end of the age. It will consist of ten confederated kingdoms, each ruled over by a king. So much the ten " horns " signify, xvii:

12. On the Dragon's heads John saw diadems. But when the Beast from the sea shall appear the diadems are transferred to the ten " horns," or ten kings, who rule in unison with the imperial head. In chap. xvii: 13, 14 we are told " they receive authority, with the beast, for one hour." " One hour " certainly does not denote mere time, a space of sixty minutes, but one and the same time. They enter into a close alliance with the Beast at one and the same time, and he and they thereby constitute in their united capacity the vast federation, the consolidated world-empire of the last days. These ten kings " give their power and their strength unto the Beast." On a worldwide scale there will then be constituted the *United States* of the prophetic earth. Such a form of government on so vast a scale has never yet been seen. But God's word solemnly predicts that there shall be. As a personal belief we may add that it will have for its center and its seat the nations of Europe, particularly those grouped around the Mediterranean sea. Out of the present European state system the coming federated Empire will be formed, though it will not be confined to these. That there are tendencies now discernible for such an international union no thoughtful person can fail to see. Our age is pre-eminently a federating age. For years the " triple Alliance " of Germany, Austria and Italy has existed. France, Spain and Great Britain stand together in support of certain Continental issues. Russia, the United States (for our country is tending manifestly toward the place and the obligations of a world-power), and even Japan of the far East, all

seem to be gravitating toward a common cause and common center. The formation of a confederate, universal sovereignty, such as prophecy clearly indicates, is not only possible, but it may be realized in few years from now.

At the head of this huge organization will stand the peerless man, the Satan-inspired man, the man in military genius and executive capacity, in intellectual brilliancy and savage ferocity, surpassing all other men. He and the Empire over which he shall rule are so thoroughly identified in the prophetic revelation as that they receive the same descriptive title, the awful name—The Beast! Three inspired prophets, Daniel, Paul and John, furnish a full description of the powers, action and end of this coming man. In Daniel he has " eyes like the eyes of a man," " a mouth speaking great things " " against the Most High;" he " does according to his will;" " magnifies himself above every god, nor regards the God of his fathers;" before him three of the horns " are plucked up by the roots;" " he wears out the saints;" and he practices and prospers for " a time, and times, and the dividing of time " (three and a half years) (vii: 8, 24, 25; xi: 36, 37).

In Thess. ii he is the " Man of Sin;" one whose inner element and outer characteristic is sin, and nothing but sin. He has a coming (*parousia*)and an apocalypse, like the Son of God. He exalts himself above all that is called God or that is worshipped. His coming is according to the working of Satan with all signs and lying wonders, and with all deceit of unrighteousness. He takes his seat in the temple of God and sets himself forth as God. *Treason against God* is his uncommon crime. In First John, ii: 22, he is the Antichrist who denieth the Father and the Son."

In Revelation (xiii: 5-8) he blasphemes God, the divine Name, the heavenly Tabernacle, and all who dwell in heaven; makes war against the saints and overcomes them; and he continues forty-two months (three and a half years). Such in brief is the portrait given by the Spirit of God of the coming Man, the Antichrist, the mock Messiah.

His origin is mysterious, apparently supernatural. Twice in the Apocalypse it is said he " ascends out of the bottomless pit," xi: 7; xvii: 8. There is something darkly significant in these words—" he cometh up out of the abyss." Some think he will be the devil incarnate; others, that he will be an ancient foe like Antiochus Epiphanes or Nero, who shall return to earth from the nether world. Many think he will be an apostate Jew. But whoever he will be or whence, one thing is certain, when he comes Satan will give him his power and his throne and great authority, will fill him from head to heel with his infernal energy, and dower him with more than human craft and cunning.

The second Beast rises from the earth, xiii: 11-18. His appearance, two-horned as a lamb, suggests harmlessness and even weakness, but his voice has in it the roar of the Dragon. His character is diabolic, and he acts in complete harmony with the other Beast, the ten-horned and seven-headed monster. This is the False Prophet, xvi: 13; xix: 19; xx: 10. The true prophet lives in God's presence and receives his messages from Him. This false prophet lives in the presence of the monster Beast, and derives all his power and authority from him. It is his business to promote the worship of the Beast and to bring the whole world into subjection to him, ver. 12. He is not an independent actor in the scenes of the End-time, he is subordinate to the first Beast, and is his servant and minister. Hence he simulates or actually works miracles, bringing fire from heaven as Elijah did at Carmel, and endowing the image of the Beast which he constructs with apparent life and speech. But let it be noted that he does not claim divine homage for himself. This the Antichrist emphatically does, as the prophets Daniel, Paul (2 Thess. ii: 4), and John (xiii: 3, 8), attest. Therefore the lamb-like beast is not the Antichrist, though in spirit and action he resembles him. He is Antichrist's " armour-bearer," as Irenæus calls him; he is his prime minister and ally.

Furthermore, he binds into a vast union or corporation all the followers of the Beast, and brands them each with his mark and number in the forehead and in the right hand, so that none may buy or sell unless he belongs to the Federation and bears the Beast's cipher—the most stupendous system of " boycott " ever established! The brand impressed on the Beast's subjects is his own name, or the number of his name, ver. 17. It seems very likely, therefore, that the name has a numerical value which is found in the addition of the letters forming the name, as most, if not all, interpreters believe. The number of the name is given as 666, a trinity of sixes, but one short of perfection. A perfect trinity of the number would be 777. Antichrist's enigmatical monagram falls short of completeness by a trine set of digits. "It is the number of a man;" that is, so far as the arithmetic goes, it is human, not that of a brute, nor of a spirit, such as the devil is: Antichrist is human, a man. What his name is or will be is absolutely unknown. Guesses there are in plenty from Irenæus' *Lateinos* down to *Napoleon*. It is useless to add others to the conjectural list. When the Beast is actually here his name with its enigmatical number will be well known; perhaps not sooner.

Here, then, are set before us sinister portraits of the foes of God and of His people of the last days: the Dragon, the Beast, and the False Prophet, a triad of diabolism. Joined with these and their dupes are countless multitudes of our poor race who shall have deliberately rejected the Gospel of the grace of God, and shall have chosen instead the strong delusion and the lie, 2 Thess. ii: 9-11; Rev. xiii: 7, 8, 12, 14, 16.

THE PROGRAM 'OF THE END, chap. xiv.

Chapter xiv contains seven visions which appear to record the main events of the closing days of our age. Chronological sequence is observed, save in the case of the first, viz.: the 144,000 with the Lamb on Mt.

Zion. This scene is anticipative and proleptic, it belongs to the consummation, and even beyond, to the Millennium itself. If the Dragon is active in ordering his forces for the final struggle, xiv: 1-5, encourages us with the assurance that the Lamb is gathering, guarding and fitting His own loyal company for the part they have in the execution of His plans. The number 144,000 no doubt is in a sense ideal, a round number, not necessarily literal, and it is made up largely, if not exclusively, of the seed of Abraham, the new Israel. That these are to be identified with the same number in (vii: 1-8) it seems certain. The number is the same; the seal of God in their foreheads there corresponds with the name of God in their foreheads here. The change from seal to name may be accounted for by the mark in the forehead and hand imposed on the followers of the Beast. God will have His ransomed ones to bear His own blessed name as their distinguishing mark. They have been redeemed from earth; they are holy and blameless; they follow the Lamb as devoted and obedient servants; and they stand with Him on Mount Zion, the earthly center for blessing for the whole race, the point of departure for the millennial kingdom and latter-day glory. They also are the firstfruits unto God and the Lamb, which means that all Israel shall be saved, for these redeemed are the pledge and sample thereof; and they are besides, as firstfruits, " the Divine kernel," as Auberlen names them, of the new humanity, the seed by which the purified earth shall be peopled.

But must we confine the 144,000 to the redeemed of

Israel? May there not be saved Gentiles among them? There is profound significance in the promise to the overcomers of the church of Philadelphia: "Because thou hast kept the word of my patience, I also will keep thee from the hour trial, which shall come upon all the world, to try them that dwell upon the earth." Safety in the hour of universal trial is here promised these saints; they are sheltered by the power of the Lord. There is no hint that a "rapture" of these from the earth takes place; the Greek preposition (*ek*) forbids the notion. The promise appears to signify that they shall be in the hour of trial, but they shall be kept in safety, and shall come out of it unscathed and untouched. So also the 144,000 of vii: 1-8; ix: 4; xiv: 1-5. These likewise are safe in the hour of trial. In the latter vision the Beast and False Prophet, the tribulation, and the suffering are all behind them; they are forever secure on Mount Zion with the Lamb. Besides, the saints in Philadelphia have Christ's name and the Father's written upon them, as the 144,000 have (Rev. iii. 12).

VISION OF WORLD-WIDE PREACHING, xiv: 6, 7.

In both the noun and verb forms of this proclamation there is the idea of glad tidings, good news—the Gospel. It is called "everlasting," both because of what it is in itself and what it promises; it is eternal as to the salvation it offers and as to the bliss it pledges. The preaching is universal, to all that dwell (Grk. *sit,* as if content with their lot) upon the earth.

Hope this preaching holds out, but it is conditional, brief. " Fear God, and give him glory; for the hour of his judgment is come." A strange Gospel surely! Judgment is impending, it is at hand, but an hour off! Therefore " fear God "—reverence, honor, obey and trust Him, for His terrific judgment is about to break down upon the guilty. It is the time of the End; the Beast, the False Prophet, the Dragon are all on the stage of action now, and the closing scenes are at hand. This is God's last, merciful appeal—His final call. It connects with our Lord's words in Matt. xxiv: 14: "And this gospel of the kingdom shall be preached in all the world as a witness to all nations; and then shall the end come."

THE FALL OF BABYLON ANNOUNCED, xiv: 8.

This is the first mention of Babylon in the book, but the seer will return to the grim topic and give us a full-length portrait of it, xvii, xviii. Here Babylon is spoken of as a corrupt and corrupting system by which the nations of earth are debauched. Her doom is announced in very striking terms: " Fallen, fallen is Babylon the great, which hath made all the nations to drink of the wine of the wrath of her fornication." Babylon's overthrow is one of the first chief events succeeding the proclamation that the hour of God's judgment is come.

Solemn Warning against any Partnership with the Beast, xiv: 9-12. The most appalling alternatives will confront men in the days when the Beast comes to the climax of his wickedness and despotism. Either men must worship him and receive his brand as being his property, or they must die, xiii: 15. Either they must utterly repudiate him and his worship and his rule, or they must suffer the awful torment prepared for the lost, xiv: 10, 11. There will be saints who will resist him to the death, xiii: 7; xiv: 12. Dreadful as will be the judgments of heaven on the apostates of that time, they will have no cause to complain, for here God in His abundant mercy, when the very end itself is in full view, appeals to men and warns them as He alone can to flee for their lives from all contact and commerce with the Beast.

BLESSEDNESS OF THOSE WHO DIE FROM HENCEFORTH, xiv: 13.

The sweetness and depth of this gracious announcement is, "henceforth," *i. e.,* from this time on. The Great Tribulation is now running its sanguinary course; the Beast has control of the world itself, and is doing his will with none to hinder, so it seems. Saints fall beneath his cruel decrees. But they, not he, are the conquerors; they die, but they rest from their toils, from their anguish and their agony (cf. vi: 11; 2 Thess. i: 7). The time of suffering is foreshortened (Matt. xxiv: 22). At the utmost it is but three years and a half, xiii: 5. But the promise in Matt. xxiv: 22 (cf. Mark xiii: 20) seems to limit even this period, so that in the case of the saints it will not run its full course; they shall be taken out of it ere the whole of it has closed. Their resurrection and glorification are near, hence they are " blessed."

THE HAVEST, xiv: 14-16.

The Reaper is none other than the Son of Man, Jesus Christ our Lord. The " white cloud " He sits on denotes it, for it is the symbol of the Divine presence. In the Transfiguration a " bright cloud " is seen. Again and again it is affirmed He will come with Clouds, " in the cloud " (Lu. xxi: 27). He wears a Crown, the Victor's Crown (*stephanos*), for now He is to show Himself the Conqueror of death and the grave. The harvest is unquestionably that of the gathering of the righteous, living and dead. Christ Himself declares that the harvest is " the consummation of the age," Matt. xiii: 39. And here the harvest is actually come, the grain is "over-ripe;" it must be gathered and garnered, for the number of the redeemed is complete, is filled up. The Royal Reaper here is the Son of God, but angels are associated with Him, as He Himself says, Matt. xiii: 39. The same supreme event is thus described by the Lord in His Olivet prediction: "And he shall send his angels with a great sound of a trumpet; and they shall gather together his select from the four winds, from one end of heaven to the other " (Matt. xxv: 31). Still another inspired account of this majestic scene is I Thess. iv: 13-18. Here is described in symbol the final and universal gathering of God's people into the everlasting Kingdom by resurrection and translation.

It occurs before the wrath of God is poured out, but not before the Tribulation, if this chapter does really present the order of events at the time of the End, as it certainly seems to do. But the harvest may be reaped before the hour of the great trial has run its course, as already intimated. Hence the comforting assurance given the martyrs in ver. 13.

The Vintage, xiv: 17-20.

This is the seventh event of the chapter, the last and the most terrible of all. It represents the wrath of God poured out to the uttermost upon the ungodly, the destroyers of the earth (xi: 18). It is the Day of Judgment, the day of vengeance, the day of the perdition of ungodly men. The figure of the vintage for this awful day of wrath is common to the prophets. Isaiah uses it of the avenging Messiah, " I have trodden the winepress alone; I will tread them in mine anger, and trample them in my fury; their blood shall be sprinkled upon my garments, and I will stain all my raiment " (Isa. lxiii: 1-4). Joel in like manner, "Come, tread ye: for the winepress is full, the fats overflow" (Joel, iii: 11, 12, 14; Rev. xix: 15); "and he treadeth the winepress of the fierceness of the wrath of Almighty God." It is the time of vengeance untempered with any mercy, wrath unmixed with any compassion, for long He has been still and refrained Himself, but now He will destroy and devour at once, Isa. xlii: 13, 14. Parallel with this judgment scene is the tremendous revelation of chap.

xix: 11-21. The event is the same in both places. The vintage here is identical with the Advent there, and with the hurling of the Beast and the False Prophet alive into the Lake of Fire, and with the slaughter of their armies.

No saints of God will be found in the winepress judgment. They are delivered from " the wrath to come " (1 Thess. i: 10): "And to you who are troubled, rest with us, when the Lord Jesus shall be revealed from heaven with his mighty angels, in flaming fire taking vengeance on them that know not God, and that obey not the gospel of our Lord Jesus Christ," 2 Thess. i: 7, 8. The prophets attest, however, that in those days of the divine judgments Israel as the chosen people will be delivered and blessed and be made a blessing, Joel iii: 17-21; Zech. xiv: 8-21. But the saints who have gone through the Tribulation will be gathered in the blessed Harvest-home safe from the devouring wrath and the consuming fire of God's vengeance.

With these closing scenes of our age as depicted in our chapter are associated the Vials of Chap. xvi. These are described as containing the seven last plagues, i. e., the divine judgments which are consummated in the End-time, " for in them is finished the wrath of God." The Vials cover the last three years and a half of the End, and they terminate with the vintage.

CHAPTER XI.

The Seven Last Plagues, xv, xvi.

Before describing the pouring out of the Vials the Seer narrates a vision of the victors at the sea of glass, xv: 2-4. The sea is of glass, not of water; it is solid; for upon (*epi*) it the victorious band stands. The figure of the glassy sea seems to be taken from the "molten sea" of Solomon's Temple (1 K. vii: 23), though with changes. "The molten sea" was for the purification of the hands and the feet of the priests; but this glassy sea is immaculate and undefilable. Those who stand upon it likewise are holy and pure, they need no washing, they have been forever cleansed from all defilement. They have come to this exalted position after trial and suffering. They have gotten victory over the Beast and over his image and over his name. Obviously they have been through the Great Tribulation. But now the scene of conflict is past. They stand, like Israel of old, on the triumphant side of the Red Sea, and they lift up their voices in exultant song. Their song is that of Moses the servant of God and of the Lamb. This fact intimates, perhaps, that they are of Jewish origin. If so, they belong to the martyred remnant referred to in xii: 11, 17. But we are not to exclude Gentile martyrs from this company on the glassy sea; perhaps we should not err greatly if we included the innumerable host of vii: 9-17 among them. They exalt God's marvellous works in their song-works of righteous judgment which He has poured upon the wicked, for they have been witnesses of their sins and crimes. They celebrate Him as " King of the ages " (" King of saints " of A. V. is no doubt wrong).

The vision is beyond question prospective, proleptic. It relates to the time when the Tribulation is past, the judgments have fallen, and God's justice has at length been fully vindicated.

The Vials (xvi) are in reality *bowls,* as the Revisors translate; they are like the cups of the Temple, broad and deep, used for pouring out the drink-offering. The Vials, of course, are figures of speech; they represent the concentrated, tremendous judgments which God will visit upon the ungodly of the End-time. Their action is amazingly swift and continuous. There seems to be no pause between them.

The Seven Plagues have affinity with the judgments inflicted on Egypt (Ex. vii: 20, 21; viii: 5, 6; ix: 15-17, etc.), and particularly with the first four Trumpets (viii: 7-12). God scourges the wicked with nature's forces as once He did the Egyptians, and as He often chastised Israel by like means. But when these Plagues are poured out the whole world will feel the fearful visitation. Earth, air, water and sun—man's beneficent servants—will then become instruments of torture and of death, and the spirits of the elements will justify God in His righteous dealings with the ungodly.

The Plagues have features peculiar to themselves.

The fourth is entirely new; the others are more intense and violent in their action than the Trumpets. The fifth deals directly with the Beast's seat of power; judicial blindness smites his kingdom; madness and defiance rule. But while men gnaw their tongues for pain and writhe in agony amid dreadful suffering, they grow more hardened and blaspheme their almighty Judge.

The sixth Vial is poured out on Euphrates. The sixth Trumpet also deals with the same river; but it sets loose the four angels bound there, who then slay the third part of men (ix: 15). Here the river is dried up so as to open the way for the coming of the kings from the sunrising. The Euphrates was the boundary and eastern limit of the old Roman Empire. In the new and satanic empire which shall arise every barrier is gone, and armies from the far East may freely pass to the place of the final struggle. The vast hordes of Asia will be involved in the decisive and overwhelming battle of the great day of God the Almighty, no less than those of other continents.

A marvellous thing happens in connection with the action of this Vial, three frog-like spirits issue from the mouth of the Dragon, of the Beast, and of the False Prophet. They are demons, vile and loathsome, yet possessed with immense power. They represent the malign influence which this devilish triad will exert over the world; it is by them that earth's armies will be organized and led into the field for the great battle with God. It is plainly said they are demons. By their persuasiveness of speech, by the

signs and wonders they will work, and by their tire-
less energy, they will lead astray the unbelieving
world, and countless hosts will march to Har-Magedon
to their awful doom. " Kings of the whole world "
shows how complete the success of these frog-like
demons will be. The earth will then be in revolt
against God. The events of the End-time will be
world-wide. A prophetic word spoken by the Lord
Jesus Himself discloses how universal the delusions
of men will be in that day: " For there shall arise false
Christs and false prophets, and shall show signs and
wonders, that they may lead astray, if possible, the
elect " (Mark xiii: 22).

The seventh angel poured out his Vial upon the air,
and a great Voice from the Throne proclaimed, " It
is done." The judgments are exhausted, the wrath is
finished.

Babylon comes into remembrance before God. In
chap. xiv: 8 the fall of Babylon is noted as the third
event in the series of the time of the End. Here its
judgment seems to be placed under the seventh Vial.
There is no real discrepancy. In chap. xvi: 17-21
the closing scenes are summed up together, and temporal sequence is not strictly observed. The great
city, and the cities of the nations, and islands, and
mountains, and Babylon, all share in the terrific judgments. Besides, chaps. xvii and xviii make it evident that the corrupt ecclesiastical system ("The
Harlot") and " Babylon " symbolize both a religious
apostasy and a city, so that it is possible that some
brief time may elapse between the overthrow of the

8.

one and of the other: the system may fall first, the
city next in the final order of the events. A precious
word in parenthesis is given us, xvi: 15: (" Behold,
I come as a thief. Blessed is he that watcheth, and
keepeth his garments, lest he walk naked, and they see
his shame.") It is for His saints. The last blows
are about to fall, but He is speedily coming now, so
watch!

Thus we come to the close of the three great sep-
tinaries, Seals, Trumpets and Vials. A kind of pro-
gression is marked by them. The opening of the
Seals reveals the events about to happen. The blasts
of the Trumpets announce the events as forthcoming.
The outpouring of the Vials execute them, and so
close the whole, God's righteous wrath being now
finished.

Once more the statement must be made that these
Visions are contemporaneous, not successive, with
long stretches of time lying between them, as the historical interpreters affirm. All three end at the same
supreme event, the Consummation, although they do
not start at the same point. The first four Seals appear to be prior to the seven years of Daniel's last
great Week, within which so mighty events are
crowded. These Seals make ready the way for those
momentous years. The remaining three Seals belong to that Week in both its halves.

The Trumpets sound during the whole of the Week,
the Woe Trumpets no doubt belong to the second half.

The Vials pertain to the second half, the final three
years and a half, the time when the Beast is doing his

worst, when the Great Tribulation is running its awful course, and wickedness and crime are at the flood. These Bowls are filled full with the wrath of God, and in them the wrath is finished, xv: 1, 7. Judgment has completed its stern work with the outpouring of the Vials.

CHAPTER XII.

The visions recorded in this great section of the book are interposed between the Vials (xvi) and the Advent of Christ, xix: 11. They are designed to furnish us with more definite and comprehensive information touching the character and the doom of Babylon the Great. Twice already has this evil system named Babylon been mentioned, xiv: 8; xvi: 19; but no explanation is there given of it. But now once more the Seer, as is his wont, goes back to open a new episode in his marvellous revelations, and he does so that he may explain what Babylon is, what its evil influence has been, and what its fate shall be. This is the theme of these chapters—Babylon the Great, the Harlot, the Mother of Abominations. Two gigantic forms of evil are made very prominent in the Apocalypse: the one is the revolt of the civil power against God; the other is ecclesiastical apostasy. The first is prefigured by the Beast; the second by the lewd Woman, the Harlot. This latter we are now to study.

1. Note the prominence of Babylon in the book, xiv: 8; xvi: 19; xvii, xviii; xix: 1-3. One chapter is devoted to the Beast, with reference to him in some others; here two whole chapters are occupied with

Babylon and the Beast, while there are references to it in three others. It is significant that it is one of the angels of the seven vials that shows John the judgment of the Harlot. As these spirits are the executors of God's wrath on the Beast, so will they be in the destruction of Babylon.

2. Descriptive names of Babylon. It is called a harlot, ver. 1. The meaning of the symbol is plain. Scripture frequently charges Israel with the sin of adultery, of playing the harlot (Ezek. xvi; Hos. i, etc.). A city also is declared to be guilty of the like sin, e. g., Jerusalem (Ezek. xvi: 2, 48). By this is meant that a people or city in relation with God who becomes unfaithful to Him, who breaks covenant with Him, who seeks after other gods, and who serves idols, is charged with the crime of spiritual adultery. Such a body is like a wife who proves disloyal to her husband and her vows, and gives her love to other men. It is one of the strongest figures the Bible uses to express God's abhorrence and reprobation of unfaithfulness to Him. The epithet, harlot, describes an apostate religious system or community. But it is noteworthy that while Israel become idolatrous is called adulteress because she is Jehovah's wife, Babylon is a harlot charged with fornication. Not once in these chapters is Babylon called adulteress, nor her sin adultery, but uniformly she is the harlot and her sin fornication. Obviously this Woman is unlike Israel in her relation with God, and must not be confounded with that people. She is not a *wife,* she may be " espoused."

Moreover, a most extraordinary name was seen inscribed on her forehead: "Mystery, Babylon the great, the mother of harlots and of the abominations of the earth," ver. 5. Whether the term " mystery " is to be regarded as a part of the inscription or an explanation of the content of the inscription is not easy to determine. Without attempting to settle which it is, let it suffice now to say that the word certainly designates the essential nature of the repulsive object on which the prophet is gazing. The fearful picture represents *Babylon,* a mysterious system, secret, fascinating and seductive in its amazing power and influence. " Mystery " is closely akin to Paul's " mystery of iniquity " (2 Thess. ii: 7) ; it stands in sharpest antithesis with " the mystery of godliness " (1 Tim. iii: 16). Wordsworth defines the term as " a secret spell bearing the semblance of sanctity."

The Scarlet Woman is also Babylon the Great. Old Babylon on the Euphrates was idolatrous, intolerant, proud, despotic. This mystic Babylon is idolatrous and fosters idolatry. She is the prolific mother of abominations. She is both corrupt and corrupting, " the Mother of Harlots." The virus of the evil system is contagious, infectious, it spreads over the earth. She is a fierce persecutor, is seen to be drunken with the blood of the saints whom she has ruthlessly slaughtered. Old Babylon was likewise intolerant and a persecutor. One instance may suffice as proof. Nebuchadnezzar, the great king of Babylon, made proclamation that " all people, nations and languages " should prostrate themselves before the golden image which he had set up. The edict was enforced by the savage threat that all who refused should be cast into a burning fiery furnace. Three Hebrews refused to worship the royal idol, and were cast into the furnace. The new mystic Babylon exhibits the like persecuting spirit, and kills all who refuse to obey her idolatrous mandates. The names inscribed on her forehead witness to her character. Israel's high priest bore a golden plate on his forehead with the ineffable name inscribed on it: " Holiness to the Lord." The Scarlet Woman bears on hers a cluster of names that brand her as most impure, most loathsome. She is both a temptress and betrayer of peoples and nations, xvii: 2, 4; xviii: 3; xix: 2. She intoxicates the world with the wine of the fury of her seductions, she drugs them with her deadly love-potions. She is presented to us as the vilest of all vile systems.

3. The place and seat that this symbolic Woman occupies are very noteworthy. She sits upon many waters, xvii: 1. The waters are explained to be " peoples, and multitudes, and nations, and tongues." The figure denotes the widespread influence which the system exerts, and the vastness of its sway over mankind. She is described as a great City, xvii: 18; xviii: 10. Babylon the Harlot, the corrupter of earth, has its seat in a city with seven hills. Furthermore, she has her seat upon the Beast, him she rules as her obedient servant. Her seat gives her a proud preeminence and insures her victorious sway. The color of the Beast is scarlet, as is the clothing of the

Woman, indicative of the blood guiltiness and perse-cutions which stain them both. The crimson-colored Beast is the same as that seen rising from the sea (xiii: 1), the blasphemous and cruel World-power. The hateful picture here given us indicates the close association the Harlot has with the godless State and her control of it. Her attire is very notable for its brilliancy and its richness; scarlet, purple, precious stones and rare gems adorn her. Her robes are im-perial, her jewels queenly. In dress and in attitude her meritricious character is displayed: " Mystery, Babylon the Great, the Mother of Harlots and of the abominations of the earth."

Such is the hideous portrait presented to us by the pen of inspiration of a corrupt and corrupting system that once had fellowship with God and labored faith-fully to further His cause among men. Now alas! it has become " the habitation of demons, and the hold of every unclean spirit, and the hold of every unclean and hateful bird " (xviii: 2). John writes: "And when I saw her, I wondered with a great wonder." It is not surprising. Who does not feel profound grief, a sense of sorrow and of awe, when looking upon the dreadful spectacle of a fallen, impure or-ganization which once was pure and true, but which now has become unfaithful and vile?

Who or what is this Woman with her twin name of Harlot and Babylon? What does the repulsive sym-bol mean? Are the predictions about her sufficiently explicit to enable us to identify her? Undoubtedly they are. More than once in the course of these notes it has been intimated that the Harlot-Babylon is an apostate religious system.   But what system is meant?

1. The Woman is sharply distinguished from the Beast.   Beyond all denial, if the Beast be the World-power, as we have all along set forth, the Woman cannot be.   She is in most intimate relations with him, but from him she is distinct.   She rides him, therefore she is not the same as he.   Before this fact the historical interpretation of the Apocalypse completely breaks down.   That view makes the Beast and the Woman the same thing—a view negatived here.

2. The Woman cannot be the star-crowned, sun-clothed Woman of chap. xii: 1, 2.   It is Israel, the Messianic nation, that is there symbolized, not at all the Christian Church.   Many interpreters, however, insist that the Woman of chap. xii and the Harlot of chap. xvii are one and the same; that she, holy and true at first, became at length degenerate and fell from her lofty estate and became at last the unclean temptress of nations and the assassin of the saints. The only real argument for the identification of the two Women we have seen is, both are found in the "Wilderness."   But the sun-clothed Woman is there sheltered from the wrath of the Great Red Dragon, and is nourished of God there for three and a half years, the period of the great tribulation.   Now, it seems to us incredible and impossible that she should become the vile and guilty Harlot of the later vision in so short a time.   The Woman of xvii is not the Woman of chap. xii become apostate.

3. The Harlot is Christendom estranged from God

and become thoroughly secularized and degenerate. This is our most solemn conviction. Romanism, we believe, is the chief subject of this frightful prophecy. But the Greek Catholic organziation, mainly as existing in Russia and Eastern Europe, as also worldly and unfaithful Protestantism are involved and included therein. We begin with the identification of Romanism with this symbol. It is official and hierarchical Romanism we are dealing with, not the body of adherents to that system who are generally both ignorant and superstitious. The historical reality and the prophetic portrait here drawn are too much alike, match too exactly, to mistake the meaning.

Papal Rome claims to be a Mother, calls herself the " mother of all churches," the mistress and teacher of all Christians. The pope asserts his supremacy over all of them, and indeed over all nations as well. In 1825 Leo XII struck a medal bearing on the one side his own image, and on the other that of the church of Rome symbolized as a Woman, holding in her left hand a cross, and in her right a Cup, with the legend, " Sedet super universum," " The whole world is her seat " (Hyslop, Two Babylons). She would dominate all mankind, xvii: 15.

The Woman has her seat in a city of seven hills, xvii: 9, 18. For more than a thousand years the Papacy and Rome the City have been regarded practically as one and the same. Rome is the Papacy to this day. No other is called "the city of seven hills;" no other has ever ruled over the earth as Rome has. Pagan Rome governed the world for centuries; papal

Rome has for ages held sway in our planet as no other city has. It is Rome where the Woman " sitteth." The city and the system coalesce, they are convertible terms.

The name inscribed on the Harlot's forehead points unmistakably to an apostate religious system, and pre-eminently to Romanism. Everything in the worship of that enormous organization is shrouded in mystery, is designed to impress men with its hidden, secret and supernatural authority and power. Its persistent use of a dead language, its celebration of the Mass, its confessional and priestly absolution, its claims to fix the destinies of men even in the unseen world, its mystic ceremonies and rites, the dress of its officiating priests and their postures and actions when observing " the mysteries " of the cult-all combine to invest the system with an impressiveness and mysticism nowhere else found save in some of the ancient pagan rites. The Greek Church is characterized by the like heathen features, though somewhat less flagrant.

The Harlot's connection with the World-power— riding upon it—is realized in the universal domination which the Papacy claims and asserts. The Pope arrogates for the Roman See supremacy over peoples and states and rulers. Not always has he been able to enforce the proud claim, but when he can he does to the fullest extent. " The pope can depose from their offices magistrates and princes, and release subjects from their oath of allegiance." " The pope is king of kings, ruler of rulers, the prince of bishops,

the judge of all men " (Bellarmino). " The imperial
majesty is subjected to the pope as the Vicar of Christ
Jesus, and kings ought to lay down their crowns before him.   The Pontiff is monarch, emperor, king and
bishop of the whole earth " (*Decisioni della Rota Ro-
mana*).   These quotations are taken from Roman
Catholic authorities; they could be multiplied indefi-
nitely.   To this day the Roman See exalts its absolute
supremacy over all nations, sovereigns and peoples.
It is not union with the State that is asserted, but dominion over the State.   Subjection to the civil authority is the position of those ecclesiastical bodies named
" State Churches," whether Protestant or Greek Catholic.   Rome exalts her authority over all States and
Churches alike.   She rides, or seeks to ride upon the
World-power, to subject to herself all authority and
all rule.

The Scarlet Woman is intolerant, persecuting: she
is seen to be drunken with the blood of the saints.
Here, again, the parallelism between the symbol and
the apostate religious system is startlingly close.
Count if you can the victims of Rome's bloody work
in the world, her murderous cruelties.   It is even
doubted whether pagan Rome ever slew as many human beings as has Papal Rome.   Nor is Rome the only
guilty one in this respect.   The Greek Catholic and
some Protestant bodies likewise have stained their
hands in the blood of some of the noblest and purest.
of God's children.   Not without a dreadful meaning
is this Harlot arrayed in scarlet and crimson: bloody-
minded she is, and blood-stained also.

The Harlot is the "mother of abominations," *i. e.*, idolatrous. Images, shrines, relics, human beings ("the saints") and angels are objects of devotion in all apostate Christendom. The Virgin Mary with vast multitudes holds a higher place of veneration than did ever Minerva in Greece, or Ceres in Rome, or Diana in Ephesus. Her worship exceeds that even of the Son of God Himself. Nothing will sooner arouse the fanatical rage of her devotees than the teaching that Mary, blessed as she was in being chosen to give birth to the Son of Man, has no part in our salvation, can do nothing to deliver us from sin and reconcile us with God. Ever since Pius IX officially proclaimed the Immaculate Conception of the Virgin, Mary has been lifted into a place of eminence and authority never before held by her. Add to this the Dogma of infallibility with which the Pope was crowned in 1870 by the Vatican Council, and one will perceive to what heights of arrogance and blasphemy this Roman system is now exalted.

But departure from divine truth, false teaching, unwarranted claims, arrogant assumptions, will worship and idolatry are not to be charged against papal Rome exclusively. Babylon is "the mother of harlots." She has daughters like herself. The Greek Catholic church, the Coptic, and others have as widely departed from the simplicity of the Gospel as has Rome. Who would venture to deny that there are signs of a falling away in Protestantism? A scarcely disguised infidelity in the great Schools of Germany; advanced ritualism and Higher Criticism of a most pronounced type advocated in the Colleges and Universities of Great Britain; scientific skepticism and rationalism taught in the Universities of our own country; " an open and organized movement toward Rome, numbering thousands of clerical and lay adherents;" in the Church of England; doctrines held and taught in Evangelical Churches that " thirty years ago would have ranked a man as an infidel;" denial of the supernatural, ridicule of miracles, denial of the inspiration, integrity, and authority of the Scriptures; hostility toward the divine claims of the Lord Jesus Christ and His Gospel; denial of the Deity of Jesus Christ, the persistent effort on the part of many to sink Him to a level with men, born into the world as other men are and having a human father and mother as other men; denial of His resurrection from the dead and His Mediatorial action in heaven as a glorified Man, and His Coming to judge the quick and the dead; Paul charged with being the author of Christianity and not Christ—a Christianity which Christ did not teach; a salvation now preached that is to be the result and fruit of " works," culture, education, " character-building," a reconstruction of society in the Socialistic conception, the importance of the individual being eliminated—all this and much more than this betokens the working of " the mystery of lawlessness" in the heart of Christendom, the presence and the corrupting influence of the Harlot's " daughters " in the " religious world." The Laodicean age, with its latitudinarianism, its proud boastings, and yet its spiritual bankruptcy ignored, has set in, though not yet full-grown. Worse things are fast approaching.

No influence for evil is so great, none so far-reaching in its disastrous effects, as an apostate religious system. There is no sphere it does not invade, none that it does not befoul. The State, the family, education, literature, the press—everything, in short, of life and of civilization it touches and defiles. Chapter xviii of Rev. discloses the vast results on mankind of Babylon's overthrow. Kings, merchants, seamen, wail over Babylon's fall, and recognize with profoundest grief that all commerce, all the immense business of the world, had hitherto been bound up with the Babylonian system, and now by the just judgment of God it has all crumbled into desolation and ruin. We believe that the predictions recorded in chap xviii involve a far wider field of influence than a single city; they point to the world of commerce, of trade—in short, to the complex, interdependent secular relations of modern civilization. Christendom does control the wealth and the commerce of the civilized nations, nay, of the heathen nations also. Babylon, the Harlot, means more than a single city, though it may have its chief place of power there. It is Rome, but likewise all that Rome stands for, all its worldwide influences. As a city Rome never was a great commercial center, nor is it ever likely to be anything like what Tyre or Alexandria were, what London and New York now are. But apostate Christendom will one day, if not now, embrace the world and poison all its centers and all its life. With Babylon's fall the complicated, rich, spectacular and cultivated civilization of earth will be utterly demolished, for in its essence and its spirit it will be the foe of God, the corrupter of the truth of God, and the righthand of the Antichrist. No wonder all heaven rejoices when the enormous thing, built up with so tremendous efforts, with such expenditure of intellectual energy, and by such unjust and evil methods, dies at length beneath the stroke of outraged justice!

The destruction of the Harlot Babylon will be by the Beast and his ten-horn confederates, xvii: 16. When the Beast has served himself of Babylon, wearied at length by its arrogance and its claims, he will turn with fury upon it, tear it to pieces, eat its flesh, devour all its wealth and its power, and burn it with fire. Two gigantic forms of full-grown Wickedness is to distinguish the time of the End. The one is, the revolt and hostility of federated Government, the other an apostate religious system. The first is not yet manifested; the second, in its incipient stage, is here.

We may summarize the intercalated Visions of chaps. xvii, xviii, xix: 1-10 thus:

1. Five world-kingdoms had flourished and fallen when John wrote.

2. The sixth Kingdom, the Roman Empire, was then existing, but was to fall.

3. A seventh Kingdom shall arise and rule the earth. Its form is to be that of a Confederation of ten kingdoms, each ruled by its own sovereign, with unity centering in its great Head, the Antichrist.

4. The Harlot Babylon the symbol of an apostate religious system.

5. Both the Beast and Babylon, as predicted in the Apocalypse, belong to the time of the end, and are prefigured as at their worst, most godless and most blasphemous.

6. Babylon is destroyed by the Beast and his ten kings.

7. The Beast and his False Prophet are destroyed by the Lord Jesus Christ.

9

CHAPTER XIII.

Advent of the Heavenly Conqueror, the Lord Jesus Christ, xix: 11; xx: 6.

1. This great section is the climax and the culmination of all the visions and predictions of the book. The Consummation so often noted in former chapters; the reiterated announcements of Christ's Coming in the seventh Seal, in the seventh Trumpet, in the seventh Vial, and elsewhere, now at last are become a reality in His personal return to our earth. The keynote has been, " Behold, He cometh." But now the diapason closes full on His Presence, " He is come." " I saw heaven opened." In chap. iv: 1 " a door is opened in heaven." Twice we are told the Temple in heaven was " opened " (xi: 19; xv: 5). But xix: 11 is on a wider scale; the heavens themselves open to the descending Son of God. He now comes, not as the Lamb, nor as the Bridegroom, but as the Lion of the tribe of Judah, the almighty Conqueror. He is followed by a dazzling retinue, the armies of heaven, His mighty angels. The scene is one of transcendant majesty. He is identified by His royal titles. He is " faithful and true " (i: 5; iii: 7, 14): " The Word of God " (Jno. i. 1): " King of kings " (xvii: 14). His personal appearance indicates who He is: " His eyes are a flame of fire " (i: 14; ii: 18); He is crowned with " many diadems," He is a King and

130

more than a king, He is above all kings and sovereigns; He is the Lord of heaven and earth: "His garment is sprinkled with blood" (Isa. lxiii: 2, 3): from His mouth issues a sharp sword (i: 16; ii: 12, 16; cf. 2 Thess. ii: 8; Isa. xi: 4). He is mounted on "a white horse," emblem of victory. This metaphor must not be confounded with the white-horse rider of vi: 2. That is a human warrior, this is the heavenly King; that is an ambitious and despotic military chieftain; this Rider judges and makes war "in righteousness." The heavenly armies that follow Him are the angelic hosts, Mar. viii: 38; 1 Thess. iii: 14; 2 Thess. i: 7-10; Jude 14; Zech. xiv: 5; Dan. vii: 10. The most momentous events ensue upon His Advent. The Beast, the False Prophet, the kings of earth and their armies are gathered to fight against the heavenly King, xix: 19. Their place of assembly is Har-Magedon, a noted battlefield (xvi: 16). Not a blow is struck by the heavenly hosts; the appearing of Christ, the great God and our Saviour, suffices to overwhelm all His foes, 2 Thess. ii: 8. The doom of the Beast and his guilty accomplice, the False Prophet, is most appalling. They were arrested, and "they twain were cast alive into the lake of fire that burneth with brimstone," ver. 20. Two men were taken to glory without passing through the gates of death, Enoch and Elijah. Two men will be flung alive into the Lake of Fire, Antichrist and his prime minister, The False Prophet. The carnage of the Beast's army is frightfully great, vers. 17, 18, 21; cf. xiv: 20. The birds of the sky are bidden to this "great supper of God,"

and they "were filled with their flesh," cf. Ezek..
xxxix: 17-20. Ezekiel predicts that it will require
seven months to bury the slain, ver. 12, of that day of
God's wrath.

This is the awful Vintage of xiv: 19, 20; cf. xix:
15—where a horseman riding over the battle-field
finds the blood of the slain bridle-deep for 1,600 furlongs! The time is, The Day of the Lord: when the
Lord Jesus shall be revealed from heaven with his
mighty angels, in flaming fire taking vengeance on
them that know not God (2 Thess. i: 7-10). It is the
time when the proud World-power in its last and dia-
bolical confederation is judged and destroyed, when
the kingdom of the world becomes the Kingdom of
our Lord and of his Christ: when " the kingdom, and
dominion, and greatness of the kingdom under the
whole heaven is given to the Son of Man and to the
people of the saints of the Most High (Dan. vii: 14,
27). It is the End of our Age, the time fully come
for the redemption of the purchased possession.

2. Satan Bound, xx: 1-3. The language of these
verses, of course, is symbolical; but back of the symbols is a glorious reality. We have here, first, the clear
recognition of the Devil's personality. He is no
myth, nor a personification of the world's evil, nor of
the principle of sin; he is a strong, fierce spirit, the
enemy alike of God and of our race and its mur-
derer (Jno. viii: 44). The names John here gives him
denote that he is a person with thought, will, character and disposition. More than twenty distinct titles
and names are given him in the New Testament,

every one of which expresses the idea of individuality and conscious being. He is as certainly an active, living spirit as is the angel Gabriel or the arch-angel Michael.

Secondly, for ages he has been unrestrained, "walking up and down in the earth," deceiving, tempting, leading captive and ruining as he listed, save as he was limited by the will of God. But, thirdly, he is now arrested and chained securely for a thousand years. The energy of the Seer's language is remarkable. Satan is " seized," next " chained;" then " cast into the abyss," after that " shut up," and finally " sealed." It is imprisonment with close confinement! It lasts for a thousand years. In chap. ix: 1, 2, the " pit of the abyss " is opened, and out of its yawning mouth issue the swarms of locusts. In xi: 7, xvii: 8 the Beast ascends from the abyss. Thrice is this undescribed Pit opened. But when the Dragon, the Old Serpent which is the Devil, and Satan, is hurled into it, securely bound with the angel's great chain, and over him in that dismal prison the huge cover shuts down, fast locked and sealed, opened no more will it be till the thousand years are finished. This will be earth's Jubilee, the longed-for Millennium. Not until Satan is seized, chained and locked up will there be, can there be, the blessed Millennium. Satan loose and a Millennium of peace and happiness are incompatible.

3. The First Resurrection, xx: 4-6.

"And I saw thrones, and they sat upon them, and judgment was given unto them: and (I saw) the souls of them that had been beheaded for the testimony of Jesus, and for the word of God, and such as worshipped not the beast, neither his image, and received not the mark upon their forehead and upon their hand: and they lived and reigned with Christ a thousand years."

This is a much controverted portion of the Revelation; it is a sort of exegetical battle-field between those who are called respectively Pre-millennialists and Post-millennialists. Into the controversy there is no intention to enter, but what appears to us to be its meaning must be set down. We have the profound conviction that a bodily resurrection is certainly affirmed by it. Three parties, we believe, are here distinguished from each other by the inspired prophet: 1, The throned assessors to whom judgment is given, who represent all the redeemed; 2, martyrs who had laid down their lives for their testimony to Jesus and to the word of God; 3, such as had refused to worship the Beast, or his image, or to receive his mark. The distinction between these classes is not one of time, for they are all alike sharers in the blessedness of the First Resurrection; nor of character, for alike they are saints of God, redeemed by the blood of the Lord Jesus Christ. Rather, the distinction is one of experience, of what had been endured and suffered by them respectively.

John first mentions those who sit on thrones, to whom judgment is given: "I saw thrones, and they sat upon them." The plural *they* is indefinite, it may denote any number. But other Scripture, it is be-

lieved, sheds light on the question who these are.
Christ Himself is certainly one here on His judgment-
throne. With Him certainly are the Apostles. "And
Jesus said unto them" (to Peter and the rest),
"Verily I say unto you, that ye who have followed
me, in the regeneration when the Son of man shall sit
on the throne of his glory, ye also shall sit upon twelve
thrones judging the twelve tribes of Israel" (Matt.
xix: 28). The "regeneration," or renewal, here
spoken of begins with the Advent of Christ and with
the resurrection and glorification of the saints, as
Paul teaches—" Creation itself shall be delivered from
the bondage of corruption into the liberty of the glory
of the children of God." It awaits the redemption of
our body, Rom. viii: 19-23. In that glorious age the
Apostles will be Christ's assessors in judging men.
But not these alone; all Christians are to be there
present and to share in judging. "Know ye not that
the saints shall judge the world?" "Know ye not
that we shall judge angels?" 1 Cor. vi: 2, 3. Here
the inspired assertion is, that the saints of God shall
judge both the world and angels. Of course, their
judgment will be in strict unison with that of Christ
Himself; but however subordinate to His it may be,
these saved men and women shall participate with the
Apostles in judgment. Their judicial action is remarkable as to extent; it includes the wicked of the
world and angels. Dan. vii: 21, 22 relates to the
same procedure—" Until the ancient of days came,
and judgment was given to the saints of the Most
High: and the time came that the saints possessed the

kingdom." The figure here as in the other cases cited is of an assize. Judgment is had, the saints are vindicated, and they come into possession of the kingdom promised. Here are included all O. T. believers.

In all these instances the time of the judicial procedure is the same; it is at the coming of the Lord in great glory and power. In union with Christ the saints as a body, the whole company of the redeemed, as we think, share with Him in judging the world and angels. The sentence, "I saw thrones and they sat upon them, and judgment was given unto them," is interpreted by the Lord Jesus, by Paul, and by Daniel, to mean the entire body of the saints, now raised up and glorified with Christ.

A distinct class of saints among the enthroned is brought to view; "and (I saw) the souls of them that had been beheaded for the testimony of Jesus, and for the word of God." Martyrs of Christ are these, believers who lay down their lives for His name and His word. " Souls " may include those " souls " seen under the altar (vi: 9), and who cried to God for vindication, and who were bidden rest and wait till their brethren and fellow-servants should be killed as they had been. It was in the disembodied state they were seen, as martyrs with the evidence of their execution on them—slain with the axe, the mode of capital punishment practiced by Rome before the establishment of the Empire. The use of the term *beheaded* seems to denote that all marytrs, whether under the Republic or the Empire, whether recent or remote, are to be included in these " witnesses of Jesus." Now they are seen as raised up and enthroned.

Still another company of sufferers are introduced: "And such as worshipped not the beast, neither his image, and received not the mark upon their forehead and upon their hand." The triumph of Christ is shared not by the martyrs only but by all who under the sway of the Beast and the False Prophet suffered reproach, imprisonment, loss of goods, maltreatment, exile. The words "such as" (*oitines*) point to a class distinct from the martyrs mentioned just before. Cyprian (fourth Cen.) noted the distinction; so do Swete, Edwards and others. John names particularly these two classes, because of their loyalty to Christ in suffering and death. Not all of them are slain, but all have the martyr spirit. Some of the last class may survive till the Advent, in which case they will be of those who shall not sleep (1 Cor. xv: 51).

Of all these disciples of the Lord Jesus, the enthroned, the martyrs, and the confessors, John says " they lived and reigned with Christ a thousand years." By the words "lived and reigned" we understand and must understand their resurrection from the dead and their "change" if alive at the Lord's coming. So John himself understood it, for he adds, " This is the first resurrection." Some 42 times this term *resurrection* occurs in the New Testament, and once with a prepositional affix (Phil. iii: 11), and in each instance its application is confined to the raising up of the dead. Hence John says, " The rest of the dead lived not until the thousand years should be finished."

Many expositors, however, deny that the passage teaches a bodily resurrection. They see in it no more than a revival of the martyr spirit and of the principles of righteousness and truth for which the martyrs suffered. With them here is announced a spiritual resurrection, and not a physical one. Let such terms be substituted for those of John, and the absurdity of the view will be quite apparent: " I saw the ' principles ' of those who had been beheaded for the testimony of Jesus; and the ' principles ' of those who repudiated the Beast; and the ' principles ' lived and reigned with Christ a thousand years. This is the first resurrection of the ' martyr spirit.' On these ' principles ' the second death hath no power. But the rest of the ' principles ' lived not until the thousand years were finished." Believe it who can that John wrote such nonsense as this, we cannot. Never once in the N. T. is the term resurrection used in this sense.

It is sometimes said that Rev. xx: 4-6 is the only passage of Scripture which teaches a distinct and separate resurrection for the righteous. If true, this should not disturb anyone. One unmistakable statement from God should convince and satisfy even the most skeptical. Matthew alone tells us that many of the dead saints arose at Jesus' death and resurrection and appeared to many in the city (Matt. xxvii: 52, 53), but does any Christian doubt it? But the assertion is not true. Other Scripture teaches that the righteous are raised up before the wicked—theirs is an out-resurrection from the dead. Isa. xxv: 7-9 and Hosea xiii: 14 point to such a resurrection. Dan. xii: 2 clearly affirms it: "And many of them that sleep in the dust of the earth shall awake, some to everlasting life, and some to shame and everlasting contempt." "Many of" does not mean *all;* the res- urrection here is not total, it is selective, many from among the whole number of the dead awake, the prophet affirms. We think Bush and Tregelles are right in translating thus: "these to everlasting life;" "those to shame," etc., and Tragelles goes on to say, "those" of the second part do not awake when "these" of the first part awake.

In Jno. v: 29 Jesus speaks of a "resurrection of life," and a "resurrection of judgment." But in ver. 24 He emphatically declares that believers "shall not come into judgment." These two resurrections ap- pear to be distinct both as to character and time. In Lu. xx: 35 the Lord speaks of a resurrection which shall be "from (*ek*) the dead," as if it were separate from that of the wicked, the righteous being taken out from among them. Paul in Phil. iii: 11 writes of his intense longing to "attain unto the resurrection from the dead." His language is very precise and emphatic. Literally this he says: "If by any means I may attain unto the out-resurrection from the dead." Paul confidently expected a resurrection for the saved as totally distinct in time from that of the unsaved; it is to be one "out from among" them. All this Scrip- ture confirms the glorious revelation in chap. xx: 4, 5 of "the first resurrection," which is confined to the saints of God, and in which the wicked do not share.

The resurrection of the holy dead takes place when
·Christ comes, 1 Cor. xv: 20, 23; 1 Thess. iv: 14-17.
At His "Shout" they are awakened, and by His
Voice they are called forth from their graves. But
here in the Apocalypse the order of events seems to be
this: (1) destruction of Antichrist; (2) imprisonment of Satan; (3) resurrection of all the righteous
dead and change of believers still living at that time
and their enthronement. But other Scripture, even
the Revelation itself, gives a somewhat different order.
We learn from 1 Thess. iv: 13-17 that the first act of
the Lord at His coming will be to raise the sleeping
saints, change living believers, and then together both
shall be caught up in the clouds to meet the Lord
in the air. They come with the Lord to the earth
as the term "to meet" imports (Lillie). Augustine
perceived this, "it is as He is coming, not abiding,
that we shall go to meet Him." As an ancient writer
expresses it, "We shall be caught away to meet Christ,
that all may come with the Lord to battle" (Am-
brosiaster). The rapture of the saints to meet the
advancing Saviour obviously is put by Paul before
the destruction of Antichrist and the binding of Satan.
In Rev. xi: 17, 18, the resurrection of the dead and
the distribution of rewards to them is placed before
the destroyers of the earth are themselves destroyed.
So, too, in the program chapter (xiv) the harvest of
the saints and their garnering precedes the awful judgment of the Vintage, xiv: 14-21. Is there, therefore,
discrepancy between the various accounts of the events
at the time of the end? There seems to be at first

sight, but it is only apparently so. In Rev. xix: 20-xx: 6 the Seer does not follow a strict chronological order. He groups the events together as if they were simultaneous (as indeed they are) without noting their succession.

Besides, prominence is here given to the doom of the great foes, the Beast, the False Prophet, and the Dragon. These have been filling the field of vision from the twelfth chapter down to this point. These horrible adversaries have been slaughtering the saints, blaspheming God, filling earth with blood and tears, with ruin and crimes, indescribable. It is fitting, it almost seems necessary and right, that their judgment and perdition should be described at once. The order is one of rank, not of time. We see the like order in Matt. xiii: 41-43, where the tares are first burned, and then the righteous shine forth in the kingdom of their Father. Yet, in point of fact, the righteous are gathered before the tares are burned, cf. Rev. xiv: 14-21. So, too, in chap. xix: 7, 8, the Marriage of the Lamb appears to precede the judgment of the Beast and the destruction of his hostile army. We believe that the Scriptures present the order of events at the Coming of Christ as follows: 1, The appearing of the Son of Man in the clouds of heaven; 2, the resurrection of the sleeping saints and the change of living believers; 3, the ascension of all the saved to meet Him in the air; 4, the descent of the Lord with His glorious retinue to earth; 5, Antichrist and his False Prophet hurled into the Lake of Fire; 6, the destruction of the hostile armies of the Beast; 7, imprisonment of Satan; 8, judgment of the nations (Matt. xxv: 31-46) ; 9, Millennial Kingdom and Glory.

"This is the first resurrection." The term " first " is to be understood numerically, and not as to rank; it marks the order of time. Is there to be a second? Unquestionably. It is described in xx: 12, 13. It is objected that it is not called the second resurrection. Neither is there mention of the first death, although the " second death " is named twice, vers. 6, 14. There is no need. In the one case *first* is understood; in the other *second* is. Before this " first " there is no resurrection named or referred to in the book, if we read it aright. For resurrection is the immediate result of the coming and presence of Jesus Christ, and as He comes in connection with this " first," and, hence, it is called first, no other has taken place. Many excellent and devout students of the Bible, however, believe that a previous resurrection has occurred, that of the Church, the Body of Christ, and they think it is set forth in the persons of the four and twenty Elders before the Throne, chap. iv. We have dealt with that passage already. Let it now be observed that if that were so, then we can see neither meaning nor force in this " first." It is a blunder. But no mistake is found in the Apocalypse. This is absolutely the first, no other in the record of the book has there been. For it is now, in these two chapters, xix, xx: 6, that Christ, " the resurrection and the life," actually appears in power and great glory. " Behold, he cometh with clouds, and every eye shall see him, and they also which pierced him; and all kindreds of the earth shall wail because of him. Even so, Amen." This majestic sentence is the central theme of the Apocalypse. Throughout the book the theme is repeated again and again. But in xix: 11ff., He visibly appears; and immediately the resurrection ensues. No resurrection precedes this of xx: 4-6.

CHAPTER XIV.

LAST REVOLT AND FINAL JUDGMENT, xx: 7-15.

Two mysterious and extraordinary events are recorded in this section. The first is, Satan's release from prison, and his last revolt and eternal doom, xx: 7-10. A thousand years work no change in his character or methods. As soon as he is set free from the abyss he begins his old habit of deceit and rebellion against the Most High, and hostility toward His people. When he was ejected from his lofty place and cast to earth (xii: 12) he had but a " short time." Now he has but a " little time," but he uses it to the uttermost in furtherance of his malignant aims. His success is marvellous. A countless throng, described as gathered from the " four corners of the earth," Gog and Magog, march against " the camp of the saints, and the beloved city." But the rebellion ends most disastrously to the rebels. Before they strike a blow the fire from heaven devours them. Their crafty and hateful deceiver is hurled into the Lake of Fire. There he encounters once more his old accomplices and dupes, the Beast and the False Prophet. They are still alive after a 1,000 years have run their course. Such is the eternal doom of Satan; we never hear of him more. Gog and Magog here must not be confounded with Gog of Ezekiel xxxviii, xxxix.

The two are quite distinct, for Gog of Ezekiel appears before the thousand years, whereas the Gog of John is after that period. Ezekiel's Gog comes from "the north," whereas this people has no definite geographical associations. The attack by the Gog of Ezekiel is connected with Antichrist, but here that great enemy has no part; he had been cast into the Lake of Fire long before this.

The second event is the Final Judgment, xx: 11-15. This transcendently majestic scene occurs after the thousand years, and after the final rebellion of Gog, and after the Devil has been cast into the Lake of Fire, "which is the second death"—how long after we are not told, and no mortal knows. Before the judgment-throne appear the dead, "the great and the small." By "the dead" we understand all our race, with the exception of those who are the blessed sharers in "the first resurrection;" all who died before the thousand years, and all who die after that period, and to the end of time, who are unsaved.

"And books were opened," *i. e.,* the records of each human life in the vast assembly were produced. That such records are kept and will be opened in due time seems evident from Psa. lvi: 8; Mal. iii: 16; Dan. xii: 1. There will be present also the book of life (iii: 5; xiii: 8; xxi: 27); for some who are saved may die during the thousand years, and their resurrection and their judgment will at this time take place. The first resurrection saints will have had theirs long before.

The rule of judgment will be "works," cf. ii: 23;

10

Matt. xvi: 27. Even in the case of Christians who have their part in the first resurrection, their manifestation before the judgment-seat of Christ will bring to light their deeds " done in the body, according to what they have done, whether good or bad " (2 Cor. v: 10).

The issue of the great trial will be, that whosoever is not found written in the book of life will be cast into the Lake of Fire.

Death and Hades will, likewise, be cast into that fearful Lake. Death, it seems, is not abolished until the Great White Throne is set up and human destiny is forever settled. With this teaching of the Apocalypse the apostle Paul agrees, for he assures us that " the last enemy that shall be destroyed is death " (1 Cor. xv: 26). Death, therefore, is not abolished even by the return of Christ, nor at the resurrection of those that are Christ's. The Advent is not a single point of time, but a period, beginning with His appearing and ending with the delivering up of the kingdom to God (1 Cor. xv: 24-28). But during the Millennial reign death will be the exception, not the rule as it now is. The prophets declare that at that time human life will be greatly prolonged, Isa. lxv: 20-22: " There shall be no more thence an infant of days, nor an old man that hath not filled his days: for the child shall die an hundred years old, and the sinner being an hundred years old shall be accursed." " Premature death, and even death in a moderate old age, shall be unknown; he who dies a hundred years old shall be considered either as dying in childhood, or as cut off by a special malediction " (Alexander). " For as the days of a tree shall be the days of my people." Some trees live for centuries; so shall be the life of the righteous in that day, saith Jehovah.

CHAPTER XV.

Vision of the City of God, xxi-xxii: 7.

Only brief notes on this great section of the book can we venture to offer. The revelation here is so transcendently sublime, so totally beyond all earthly knowledge and experience, that adequate interpretation is impossible; we must wait till we shall see its accomplishment to form just conceptions of its surpassing grandeur and beauty.

1. It is announced there shall be a new heaven and a new earth; and there shall be no more sea. The fulfilment of this wonderful prediction will involve a fundamental change in the physical constitution of the world that now is and also of the visible heavens. Life would be impossible if the sea was "no more." Other Scripture gives assurance of the like transformation of the physical universe with which we are connected. "For, behold, I create new heavens and a new earth: and the former things shall not be remembered, nor come into mind," Isa. lxv: 17 (cf. 2 Pet. iii: 5-13). He who made the world and all it contains can surely re-create it, clearing it of every vestige of sin and misery, of its limitations and its imperfections, and fitting it for the dwelling of perfect beings and of God's supreme glory. John is bidden, Write, for these things are true and faithful; they shall not fail to come to pass.

148

2. Descent of the new Jerusalem into the glorified earth, i: 2-4. The wicked and apostate system that once flourished had its capital city, Babylon. The pure and holy world is to have its bright and happy Capital, the new Jerusalem which comes out of heaven from God. In it will be the Shekinah, the Divine Presence, of which the glory in the Tabernacle and in the Temple was but a faint shadow, a dim reflection. He will dwell with the blessed inhabitants of the fair City —the ultimate fulfilment of all that lies hidden in the name, Immanuel. It will be in reality the sorrow-less state, painless bliss, deathless life. Think how great a chasm would be made in our English tongue if all the words telling of grief and suffering, of tears and sobs, of pain and death, were stricken from it! No such terms will find a place in the language of the new Jerusalem, for the miseries and woes which give them birth will never be known there. " God shall wipe away every tear from their eyes." He will expunge the very fountain of tears. There will be nothing in the surroundings to call forth tears, there will be no capacity in the saved to weep. The eighth verse describes those who shall have no share in the bliss. The " fearful " means the cowardly, those who like craven soldiers turn their backs and flee when they encounter the enemy-apostates, in short. To these are joined the faithless, the abominable, murderers, fornicators, sorcerers and liars. Only " he that overcometh " shall possess this infinite heritage.

3. Description of the Heavenly City, xxi: 9-xxii: 5. This section gives us a nearer view of the Holy

City. It is very noteworthy that the view was given John through the ministry of one of the angels of the Seven Vials. It was one of these same angels who showed him the "judgment of the great harlot," xvii: 1. It was fitting that he who had furnished the vision of the ungodly and apostate city, should present the Seer with the vision of the Heavenly City.

(a.) Its Structure and Dimensions, xxi: 9-17. John's point of view is that of "a mountain, great and high," ver. 10. Ezekiel (xlii: 2ff) was also set upon a mountain when he was shown "the frame of a city" —a vision which corresponds in some degree with this of John, and which probably refers to the same thing. The descent here mentioned is identical with that of ver. 2. He returns to the subject now to give a fuller description. The first thing that arrests his attention is the City's flashing light, "Her light was like unto a stone most precious, as it were a jasper stone, clear as crystal." The term "light" is peculiar; not light in the abstract, but a body of light, as a star, a blazing luminary. The whole great City glowed with a light as a mighty sun. Crystaline and smoke-less flame was the brilliant splendor with which it shone. Gems of the rarest and purest quality, gold that is transparent like the finest glass, are the only symbols which even an inspired prophet can use to set forth its majestic glory.

The Wall surrounding it had twelve foundations containing the names of the twelve Apostles of the Lamb, ver. 14, and these were garnished with "all manner of precious stones." Twelve gems are mentioned as adorning the foundations. Swete writes that the stones " in the main are of four colors, viz.: blue (sapphire, Jacinth, amethyst), green (Jasper, chalcedony, emerald, beryl, topaz, chrysoprasus), red (sardonyx, sardius), yellow (chrysolite)." All this tends to deepen and clarify the conception of the exquisite beauty, the dazzling glory, the preciousness and wealth of the Heavenly City.

The City lies four-square, is a perfect cube. Its encompassing wall is pierced by twelve Tower-gates, whereat twelve angels are stationed as royal guards or keepers. The gates have the names of the twelve tribes of Israel. Three gates are found in each side of the squares, each is a pure pearl. The combination of the twelve tribes of Israel and the twelve Apostles of the Lamb appears to signify the unity and the totality of the redeemed, both of Israel and of the Christian Body. All distinctions of race, creed and age will be unknown in the Holy City.

The wall's height is given as 144 cubits, probably equalling 216 feet. Its height is exactly the square of twelve. The length, breadth and height are equal (ver. 16), and they measure 12,000 *stadia*. A *stadia* is given as 606¾ feet, and the whole would be the stupendous sum of nearly 1,400 English miles.

(b.) Its Sanctuary, Light, Riches and Inhabitants, xxi: 22-27. It has no Temple as had the earthly Jerusalem; God and the Lamb are its Temple. Worship will not need any ceremony or rite, ritual or sacred place, in order to be earnest and wholehearted. Nothing will thrust itself between the soul and Him who is loved; fellowship will be direct and unbroken.

The City's light will be the Lord's radiant presence. It will need neither sun nor moon. The Lord's infinite glory will be its light. It will be forever safe, its gates will never be shut, its riches secure, its holiness unstained and untarnished by any breath of impurity.

(c.) Its perfect bliss, xxii: 1-5. Paradise is finally and forever restored.

THE EPILOGUE, xxii: 6-21.

The Prologue is chap. i: 1-8, eight verses; the Epilogue contains sixteen verses, twice as many. The Coming of the Lord is the pre-eminent theme of both. In the Prologue we have these majestic words: " Behold, he cometh with clouds, and every eye shall see him, and they which pierced him; and all kindreds of the earth shall wail because of him. Even so, Amen." But this, sublime as it is, is surpassed by the threefold testimony of the Advent in the Epilogue. " Behold, I come quickly: blessed is he that keepeth the sayings of the prophecy of this book," xxii: 7. "And behold, I come quickly; and my reward is with me to give to every man as his work shall be," xxii: 12. " He that testifieth these things saith, Surely I come quickly; Amen. Even so, come, Lord Jesus," xxii: 20.

There are seven " blessings " pronounced on those who do or suffer certain things. They are:

I. i: 3; blessing on him who reads and they who hear the words of the prophecy of this book.

2. xiv: 13; blessing on the dead who die in the Lord from henceforth, for the Lord is speedily coming, they shall be raised up in the power of an endless life.

3. xvi: 15; blessing on him who watches and keeps his garments, for the Lord is coming as a thief, swiftly, suddenly.

4. xix: 9; blessing on him who is called to the marriage supper of the Lamb.

5. xx: 6; blessing on him who has part in the first resurrection.

6. xxii: 7; blessing on him who keeps the sayings of this book, the Lord is at hand.

7. xxii: 14; blessing on him who has washed his robes that he may enter into the Holy City, R. V.

A special woe is denounced against him who shall tamper with the book's contents, xxii: 18, 19. Words such as these are not attached to any other book of Scripture (cf. Deut. iv: 2; xii: 32), and they guard with jealous urgency its integrity, and solemnly warn against any mutilation of it; for the Apocalypse is God's, divine, perfect, closed, certified and signed not only by the apostolic name, " I John," but the far greater name, " I Jesus." It is attested as no other is in all the Bible. How reverently and honestly and earnestly it should be read and studied.

Made in the USA
Middletown, DE
13 September 2024

60859588R00091